THE WISDOM OF THE WISE

THE WISDOM OF THE WISE

THREE LECTURES ON FREE TRADE IMPERIALISM

BY

W. CUNNINGHAM, D.D., F.B.A.

FELLOW AND DIRECTOR OF ECONOMIC STUDIES IN TRINITY
COLLEGE, CAMBRIDGE; FORMERLY TOOKE PROFESSOR
OF ECONOMICS IN KING'S COLLEGE, LONDON,
AND LECTURER ON ECONOMIC HISTORY
IN HARVARD UNIVERSITY.

CAMBRIDGE:
AT THE UNIVERSITY PRESS
1906

CAMBRIDGE
UNIVERSITY PRESS

University Printing House, Cambridge CB2 8BS, United Kingdom

Cambridge University Press is part of the University of Cambridge.

It furthers the University's mission by disseminating knowledge in the pursuit of education, learning and research at the highest international levels of excellence.

www.cambridge.org
Information on this title: www.cambridge.org/9781107433137

© Cambridge University Press 1906

First published 1906
First paperback edition 2014

A catalogue record for this publication is available from the British Library

ISBN 978-1-107-43313-7 Paperback

IN MEMORY

OF

Prof. Sir J. R. SEELEY.

PREFATORY NOTE.

TO try to take opponents at their best seems to be a sound maxim of controversy. These lectures, which were delivered in Cambridge last term and repeated in Edinburgh and Glasgow during the Easter vacation, have been called forth by the utterances of recognised leaders among Free Trade Imperialists. To Tariff Reformers the wisdom of these wise men is not altogether convincing, though we go further with them than they seem to suppose. With Mr Strachey, indeed, we have little in common; but, in discussing our attitude to Economic Science, Mr Haldane has been curiously successful in blessing where he meant to ban; and Lord Rosebery, while speaking on the case of the Unemployed, has thrown out a suggestion which we are eager to put into effect.

I have added two appendices on cognate matters to which I could only refer in the lectures, and with which I had already dealt more fully. I desire to make my grateful acknowledgment for the valuable suggestions I have received while preparing these lectures from Dr L. Knowles of the London School of Economics; and also to Messrs Macmillan for their kindness in allowing me to reprint an article which originally appeared in their *Magazine*.

W. C.

TRINITY COLLEGE, CAMBRIDGE.
13 *April*, 1906.

CONTENTS.

PAGE

I.   THE RIGHT HON. R. B. HALDANE AND
     ECONOMIC SCIENCE   1

II. MR ST LOE STRACHEY AND IMPERIAL SENTI-
     MENT   33

III. LORD ROSEBERY AND THE UNEMPLOYED   .   63

APPENDIX.

RELIGION AND POLITICAL LIFE   91

THE IMPERIALISM OF CROMWELL   106

THE RIGHT HON. R. B. HALDANE

AND

ECONOMIC SCIENCE.

The allegation that Tariff Reformers discard Economic Science altogether.

I. The strength of the Classical Economists in clearness of thought.

II. The defects of the Classical Economists in their treatment of practical problems.

III. The possibility of progress in Political Economy as an empirical and historical science.

THE RIGHT HON. R. B. HALDANE

AND

ECONOMIC SCIENCE.

THE House of Commons is an excellent institution when it attends to its own business, but it does not show to advantage when it assumes the right to give an authoritative explanation of current events. There was a curious instance at the beginning of last century, during the period when cash payments were suspended and the Bank of England was not under an obligation to meet its notes with gold. A Bullion Committee had been appointed to enquire into the state of the currency; they reported that the notes of the Bank of England were depreciated as a matter of fact, while they also pointed out the steps that were necessary for a restoration of the currency. But these proposals, which were unpalatable to the majority of the House, were defeated after a long debate. Not content with this victory, the Commons proceeded solemnly to give an authoritative—though entirely mistaken—explanation of the condition of the currency. Mr Canning pointed out that little weight would attach to this pronouncement[1], but the ministers were not to be gainsaid. As a writer on banking relates,—Mr Vansittart, "in the plenitude of his power and party strength and in the mere wantonness of tyranny, determined to drag the House through the lowest depths of ridicule and absurdity[2]." This incident does not stand quite by itself; perhaps the historian of the future may be inclined to criticise Sir Henry Campbell Bannerman's determination to put on record the official opinion that "in the recent General Election the people of the United Kingdom have demonstrated their unqualified fidelity to the principles and practice of Free Trade." We do not grudge the members of the Liberal· party the pleasure of congratulating one another on their success; but we still remember that the total numbers polled show that a considerable percentage of the electors are dissatisfied with our present fiscal system. The Labour party, though they have no confidence in Mr Chamberlain's proposals, occupy a somewhat detached position, for they refuse to pin their faith to the principles of Free Trade[3]. There were, moreover, some contests that were very significant, not only those where the judgment of bye-elections was reversed, but also

---

[1] This was especially true of the Third Resolution, 13 May, 1811. Hansard, xx. 95.

[2] McLeod, *Theory and Practice of Banking*, II. 53.

[3] Mr Keir Hardie, M.P., *The Labour Party, its aims and policy* in *National Review*, Feb. 1906, p. 1006. Mr P. Snowden, M.P., in the House of Commons, *Times*, 13 March, 1906.

those for the University seats,—Cambridge, Glasgow and Aberdeen, Edinburgh and St Andrews, and London. In all these cases, whether he was sitting member, or whether he attacked the seat, the Free Trader was defeated. Mr Strachey and Mr Murison may regret that they did not assault some other strongholds; Sir Michael Foster's eminent position in scientific circles did not save him; and Sir John Gorst, despite the support he received from the Cambridge University Free Trade Association and the strong college esprit-de-corps which rallied round him, was beaten by a handsome majority. There is some ground for saying that these elections go to show that Free Trade no longer satisfies the educated classes; they have not abandoned it, but they are not prepared to maintain it at all costs. They feel that the familiar formula is arid and uninspiring; and so, the blind confidence, with which Free Trade was accepted some few years ago, has been rudely shaken.

There is, however, one point that weighs with many men, and renders them disinclined to trouble themselves about the Fiscal Question. They suspect that, though the suggestion of Imperial Preference and Retaliation is plausible, it must somehow be unsound. They feel that it is a matter of extreme difficulty, since the argument turns on details with which they are unfamiliar and with the interpretation of statistics. Distrusting their own powers in the matter, they are inclined to attach great importance to the opinion of experts; and they know that the leading professors of Political Economy spoke strongly against the dangers of altering our present system in their manifesto to the *Times* in August, 1903. In spite, however, of the weight of the names attached to that memorial it can hardly be said that expert opinion, even in England, is unanimous on the subject. Among the best known economic works published during the last fifteen years have been Mr Booth's investigations into the conditions of London, Mr and Mrs Webb's *Industrial Democracy* and *History of Trades Unions*, and Mr Inglis Palgrave's *Dictionary of Political Economy*; and these authors have not endorsed this manifesto. We may note that the names of Professor Foxwell, the keenest student of the history of economic doctrine, of such statisticians as Sir Robert Giffen and Mr Schooling, of an historian like Prof. Ashley and of a sociologist like Mr Kidd are absent. My friends Professor Nicholson and Mr Bowley are distinguished by their vigour—both as writers and teachers ; but with these exceptions it may be said that the economists who are best known for their literary activity as investigators have not associated themselves with the professors who are mainly occupied in expounding recognised doctrines.

The fact remains, however, that in the United Kingdom the most eminent professors and instructors are opposed to fiscal change. But after all, this is not conclusive; it frequently happens, in literary and artistic circles, that the members of some little coterie succeed in establishing themselves for a time as the arbiters of taste. They review one another's books, and appreciate one another's work, and create one another's reputations, till the public come to take them seriously. Intellectual sympathy in scientific pursuits is not so likely to lead to the formation of such coteries; but a group of this kind attained great importance in Paris, at a time when Adam Smith was living in that city. The Physiocrats, or Economists as they called themselves, had a good deal of influence on the fiscal policy of the day, but their reputation has not been very lasting. Adam Smith was rather contemptuous of a doctrine which existed "only in the speculations of a few men of great learning and ingenuity in France"; he did not think it worth while to expose the errors of this system at length. "As men are fond of paradoxes, and of appearing to understand what passes the comprehension of ordinary people, the paradox which it maintains concerning the unproductive nature of manufacturing labour has not perhaps contributed a little to increase the number of its admirers." "This sect," as he adds, "in their works, which are very numerous...all follow implicitly and without any sensible variation the doctrine of M. Quesnay....The admiration of the whole sect for their master, who was himself a man of the greatest modesty and simplicity, is not inferior to that of any of the ancient philosophers for the founders of their respective systems[1]." M. Say condemns them more vigorously. "By their sectarian spirit, by the dogmatic and abstract language of most of their writings, by their tone of inspiration, they

[1] *Wealth of Nations*, IV. ix. p. 282.

make it appear that all those who have investigated economic questions were impracticable dreamers[1]." With this instance before us, we may be doubtful whether any group, however eminent, of teachers in England have really a right to speak for Economic Science as a whole, or whether they may not be merely a coterie like that of the French economists. When I had the opportunity of spending a little time in America, I found I had got beyond the sphere where the influence of this English school dominates; and the opinion of French and German experts should not be left out of account, if an attempt is made to express the judgment of Modern Economic Science on the points at issue. I do not pretend to say what the opinion of the whole scientific world may be; I think it quite likely that many foreign professors, unlike the English coterie, feel unable to pronounce on the subject off-hand, and prefer to study it first and write afterwards. But some of them have examined the question with care, and we know the results they have reached. There are two professors at Berlin, who belong to somewhat different schools of thought; but they have come to very similar conclusions on this matter. "If Mr Chamberlain attains his object," says Professor Schmoller, "especially in drawing Canada and Australia into closer relations with the mother country, he will have laid the foundations of English power anew[2]." Professor

---

[1] J. B. Say, *Discours Préliminaire* to *Traité d'économie politique*, I. p. lii.

[2] *Grundriss der Volkswirthschaftslehre*, II. 641.

Wagner takes a similar view, though, unlike his colleague, he does not regard the prospect with complete equanimity, so far as German interests are concerned. He holds that "the carrying out of Mr Chamberlain's scheme would be exceedingly favourable for England[1]." The approval which was given in anticipation by Dr Fuchs, who made a special study of the whole subject some years ago, is even more remarkable[2]. On the other hand, M. Blondel, while he recognises how rapidly England is losing her industrial supremacy[3], is doubtful as to the benefit of a change which he regards as imminent[4].

Enough has been said to show that Economic Science, as cultivated throughout the world, is at all events divided on the subject. The plain man is hardly justified in accepting the opinion of the English academic coterie as final; he is called upon to try and consider, so far as he can, what their opinion on this question of practical politics is worth.

Free Traders have not only been inclined to shelter themselves behind this academic authority, but they have also attempted to raise a prejudice against those of us who are unconvinced by the Fourteen Professors, as if Tariff Reformers rejected scientific methods altogether. In the address on

[1] Preface to M. Schwab, *Chamberlain's Handels politic*, p. viii.

[2] *Trade Policy of Great Britain*, p. 388.

[3] M. V. Bérard, another of Mr Chamberlain's critics, does not conceal his satisfaction over England's relative decline, *L'Angleterre et l'Impérialisme*, p. 380.

[4] *La politique) protectionniste en Angleterre un nouveau danger pour France*, pp. 63, 106.

Modern Logicians and Economic Methods, which Mr Haldane delivered to the Scottish Society of Economists, he complains that "during the two years which have just gone past, a good many people have written, and still more have spoken" as if they imagined that "the characteristic categories of the old economists belong properly to the lumber room[1]." Though he exempts me from this accusation, he still seems to think that the language which I used about the Classical Economists, in my address as President of the Economic Section of the British Association at Capetown[2], was unduly disparaging[3]. But the suggestion that we discard scientific treatment is a charge which we repudiate altogether; the matter is far too difficult to be dealt with properly by crude common sense, or in a dilettante fashion. We fully realise the importance not only of clear thinking, but of hard study as well. It is worth while to spend a little time in considering the lines on which such thorough investigation must proceed; and to try to see how far we should be content to follow the great writers of the past, and in what ways modern science may claim to have advanced beyond their standpoint.

I. In the paper from which I have already quoted, Mr Haldane has given us an admirable statement as to the great excellence of the Classical Economists.

[1] *Economic Journal*, xv. 502.

[2] *Journal of the Royal Statistical Society*, Jan. 1906.

[3] "With deference to Dr Cunningham," he writes, "it is probable that the Classical Economists knew pretty well what they were about." *Loc. cit.* 501.

"They taught men to think clearly, and their books are admirable illustrations of the strength as well as the weakness that is characteristic of every kind of scientific method[1]." To me the service which they rendered in this way seems quite invaluable; they have presented us with such clear ideas of money, and the instruments of exchange, and of the meaning of rent and other payments made by way of exchange, as to provide us with a convenient terminology for discussing economic questions with precision. No one, who has given attention to economic literature in what we may call the pre-scientific era, can fail to be struck with the extraordinary advance in accuracy of statement and clearness of reasoning which was brought about by their use of an abstract method. In this connection it may suffice to quote some of Mr Haldane's admirable sentences on the nature of science in general, and of Economic Science in particular. "All science proceeds by abstraction; all abstraction takes place by exclusive attention under the guidance of particular conceptions or categories[2]."…"Consideration of the true nature of economic method seems to show that it is no more open to criticism than are the methods of mathematics and physics. All three are abstract in the sense of shutting out, in order to gain clear knowledge, all aspects which are not relevant to the immediate purpose[3]." The creation of economics as a science dates from the time when Adam Smith called ex-

[1] *Economic Journal*, xv. 501.
[2] *Loc. cit.* 497.　　　　　[3] *Loc. cit.* 500.

clusive attention to the idea of Value-in-exchange,
and rendered it possible to pursue an abstract method,
in the sense of shutting out, in order to gain clear
knowledge of that which has value-in-exchange, all aspects which are not relevant to the immediate purpose.
This was the task on which the Classical Economists
entered; they analysed the idea, and worked out its im-
plications. They have given us particular conceptions
and categories, under the guidance of which we can
classify the results of our observation and build up
a coherent body of knowledge within the limits we
lay down for ourselves. Mr Haldane seems to me
to call attention to the gist of the matter when he
insists that "all that we can legitimately require"
from the economist or any other man of science is
"that he should remember that his method is
abstract[1]."

The writings of the Classical Economists are a
model for all time just because they were so careful
to remember that their method was abstract; there
was no doubt, and no confusion about it; and this
although their mode of treatment underwent considerable changes. Adam Smith had laid stress on
the notion of exchange-value, and this was the particular conception, or category, under the guidance
of which Ricardo and James Mill and Macculloch
pursued their excellent researches. But the great
investigation which Malthus conducted into the
question of population, not only had a profound

---

[1] *Economic Journal*, xv. 502.

influence on the manner in which men regarded
some practical problems, but affected the habits of
mind of scientific economists. Malthus had engaged
in a great inductive sociological enquiry, and based
the principles he enunciated on evidence drawn from
all parts of the globe; he followed out the influence
and tendency of one dominant motive in human
nature. Under the impulse which he gave, economists became more inclined to regard their science
as tracing out the influence of another great motive
in human nature,—the desire of wealth. There has
been a certain amount of loss in turning attention
so directly on subjective factors, rather than on the
external phenomena of wealth, but we have gained
in the clearer conception attained of the nature of
economic forces. Mill concentrated attention on the
desire for wealth as a dominant force; but he did
not attempt to establish the universal character of
this motive by an inductive process. It is notorious
that among many savage races, its influence has been
completely counteracted by the pleasure of pure idle-
ness; while it has little free play in highly organised
communities where there is any sort of caste system,
and the desire for social status is more powerful than
that for mere wealth. Induction from observed fact
was not possible in this case as it had been with
Malthus; but it seemed perfectly legitimate to
get at the principle in another way,—by analysing
the character of the typical man in modern progressive communities. The desire of wealth is the
dominant motive in the " economic man"; it is per-

fectly legitimate to shut out all aspects, which are
not relevant to the immediate purpose, in order to
gain clear knowledge of the probable action of the
economic man, and therefore of the tendencies which
are at work in a community in which many individuals approximate to this particular type. This
method was clearly expounded by Mill, in an essay
written about 1830; and it was brilliantly defended
by Bagehot as late as 1876. " It assumes that every
man who makes anything makes it for money, that
he always makes that which will bring him in most
at least cost, and that he will make it in the way
that will produce most and spend least; it assumes
that every man who buys, buys with his whole heart,
and that he who sells, sells with his whole heart, each
wanting to gain all possible advantage. Of course
we know that this is not so, that men are not like
this; but we assume it, for simplicity's sake, as an
hypothesis [1]." This mode of procedure was, as it
seems to me, thoroughly scientific; it was abstract;
but then, there was very little difficulty in re-
membering that the reasoning was of an abstract
character.

[1] Bagehot, *Economic Studies*, p. 5. The origin of the phrase
Economic Man has not been traced either in Dr Murray's *Diction-
ary* nor in Mr Inglis Palgrave's. Prof. Nicholson, writing in 1878
(*Machinery and Wages*, p. 18), quotes from Thompson, an Ameri-
can writer, a sentence in which it is used as a well-known term.
The consumer "is an innocent *ens logicum* manufactured by the
same process of abstraction by which the economists derived their
Economic Man, a 'covetous machine impelled to action only by
avarice and the desire for progress.'" *Social Science and National
Economy*, p. 269.

The best safeguard against forgetting the limitations under which such reasoning proceeds lies in a clear statement of the assumptions which it involves: the Classical Economists were at pains to make it clear that they took for granted certain conditions and circumstances, so as not to be distracted from the precise enquiry they had in hand. In this form the reasoning of the economists attained the highest degree of certainty; it was demonstrably true; they argued that on the supposition of certain premises, a particular conclusion would follow. Such argumentation only becomes dangerous when there is any uncertainty as to what elements are taken into account; those who are not at pains to state their assumptions clearly, may be uncertain themselves or leave others in doubt as to the precise conditions within which their argument holds good, and thus deceive themselves as to the range within which their principle applies, and the force which it ought to have. There is abundant scope for the misuse of abstract reasoning on the part of those who are not aware how abstract it is.

From a purely scientific standpoint it is, I think, a matter of regret that this abstract treatment has been so generally abandoned. We are commonly told by ecclesiastical historians that the original purity of Christian teaching was tainted when it came in contact with pagan habits of thought and worship; and there certainly does seem to have been a departure from the clearness and accuracy of economic reasoning when attempts were made to

render it more popular.   M. Bastiat, a French
Economist, was a pioneer in this direction; he was
eager to present the truths of Economics in a form
in which they would give an easily apprehended
reply to socialism.   He held that there is an economic
harmony in the world, so arranged that each man, in
the effort to satisfy his own wants, makes the most
effective contribution of which he is capable to the
good of the world as a whole[1].   This view rested on
a belief in Divine Wisdom as controlling the Universe.   Economics was still an abstract science, for a
hard and fast line was drawn between man as an
economic unit, and man as a member of Civil Society.
Bastiat held that, in the former capacity, the free
action of individuals tended to what is best on the
whole; and hence with him, Economics was no longer
a Science following out the course of certain tendencies, but almost a branch of Ethics describing
what ought to be done for the general well-being[2]
Whatever advantages there may have been in this
mode of presentation, it did not tend to clearness of
thought. Bastiat's writings gave rise to the impression,
which still seems to hold good, that *laissez faire* and
Free Trade are in some sense a virtuous course of
action, closely related to the teaching of the Sermon
on the Mount.   Through his friendship with Cobden,
Bastiat's writings came to be well known in English

---

[1] *Harmonies of Political Economy*, translated by P. J. Stirling,
2nd ed., p. 339.

[2] Dr Aubry follows the economic as well as the political views
of Bastiat in his *Étude Critique*, p. 184.

circles. Men who could not accept his sociological views, were yet inclined to break away from the strict scientific tradition, in the hope of thereby laying popular misconceptions at rest. The public do not appreciate the importance of abstract reasoning on economic affairs, and they never could remember that it was abstract. They assumed that Political Economists held up the "economic man" as an example of what all men ought to be, and insisted that the teaching of the science was sordid and its ideals low. Hence, Professor Marshall has been tempted to discard the economic man[1]; Bastiat asserted that the Ethical and the Economic were blended in the scheme of the world as a whole, and Professor Marshall insists that they are mingled, in varying proportions in different groups of mankind. He is prepared to examine the regular play of motives of many kinds in an ordinary human being. Whatever advantages there may be in this modification, there is at least a great loss of clearness; for it is impossible to say definitely what assumptions are made, and thus to make evident how far the reasoning is abstract, and what bearing it has upon actual life. If we get rid of the apparent harshness of the classical form of the science, we also get rid of all its precision. Instead of taking the individual we know in business communities, we are forced to take "mankind in the mass," and to try to analyse the main motives which sway people in general.

[1] *Principles of Economics*, p. vi.

There may be some doubt as to the method by which we arrive at our conception of the ordinary man, whether it is by introspection, or by induction from a world-wide survey. In any case the science thus presented is imperfectly abstract, since we have no means of stating clearly what is assumed, either in regard to man individually or as to society. The economic man, with all his faults, was a convenient reminder to us of the nature and limitations of the reasoning in which he appeared. What we may require of the man of science is "that he should remember his method is abstract"; but Economics in its more genial form, as commonly taught in England, has become very imperfectly abstract, because what it leaves out of account cannot be clearly stated. It is, if we may apply Mr Haldane's happy phrase, merely "a hybrid science."

As one result of the confusion that has thus been introduced into the abstract science of the Classical Economist, we are left in doubt as to the kind of validity which attaches to Economic reasoning. Mr Haldane himself does not make clear what place he would assign to Economics in the circle of the sciences. On one hand he ranges it with mathematics and physics, as if it were an abstract science in the strictest sense, and its reasoning were demonstrative in character ; on the other hand, he speaks of it as if it were an empirical science, and its results were dependent on observation and induction. "It can only deal," he says, "with tendencies and probabilities—probabilities which become certainties, only

when a wide-enough area is surveyed[1]." When Mr
Haldane fails to keep the distinction clear, there is no
reason for surprise that less skilful thinkers should
fall into positive confusion, and occasionally write
as if their reasoning had a demonstrative character
which does not really attach to it. It is a pity to
allow oneself habitually to speak more positively than
the information available warrants.

Another defect of the hybrid science lies in the
difficulty of applying its conceptions to some of the
most important phenomena of modern economic life ;
since it deals with the subjective play of motives, it is
an individualistic rather than a social science. Social
action and collective bargaining are among the most
interesting features of our day, and it is inconvenient
to approach them from the individualistic point of
view. The play of motives only explains individual
action, and there is a certain awkwardness in applying
it to corporate and collective action. Tendencies
which are more or less the tendencies of every individual are, as Mr Haldane assures us, "everywhere
operative," but this statement takes us a very little
way in seeing how they operate, or in understanding
the action of the various societies and corporations in
a highly organised community. Personal utility or
disutility may explain why a man joins a Trade
Union, but does not directly account for the action
of the Union as a body.

There is a further difficulty in attempting to
verify any of the conclusions of this hybrid science ;

[1] *Economic Journal*, xv. 501.

we cannot tell whether the reasoning is merely in the air, or within what limits of place and time it is supposed to apply. Those who rely, in their investigations of economic phenomena, on principles which do not rest on observation and induction, but are derived from subjective analysis, discard all known safeguards against hasty generalisation. From every point of view we may see that this hybrid science fails in the very point in which the Classical Economists were conspicuously successful, since it encourages slovenly thinking. The hybrid science, which has been developed on English soil on the impulse given by Bastiat, is cumbrous and confused[1], and its exponents have lost themselves in a fog from which they are unable to escape. At all events, they are not able to help the public towards a mental attitude in which it is possible to discuss economic problems thoroughly and effectively.

II. The lasting importance of the Classical Economists is due to the fact that they afforded help to those who wish to think clearly on complex social problems; but the method they pursued had, as Mr Haldane acknowledges, some "weakness," or, as I should prefer to say, had limitations. The principles they detected were not readily applicable

---

[1] This criticism has been published, in a somewhat extended form, in my *Plea for Pure Theory*, read before the London Economic Club (*Economic Journal*, 1890), as well as in *Back to Adam Smith*, read before the Scottish Economic Association in Dec. 1903 (*Rise and Decline of the Free Trade Movement*, 2nd ed., p. 190).

to the affairs of life. Political Economy, in its strictly scientific character, as an abstract science which investigates tendencies, could not offer any guidance in actual difficulties. In order to give our reasoning a practical character, we must have clearly before us some aim which we ought to pursue, or which it is expedient to pursue. As a scientific study of phenomena, Political Economy cannot lay down the end towards which men at any place or time ought to direct their efforts; it is only when some aim has been generally accepted and recognised as worth striving after, that Economic Science can come in to suggest the means by which it may be attained. In so far as the Classical Economists departed, as they occasionally did, from the examination of tendencies, and made an incursion into practical politics, they were unfortunate, because they did not appear "to know what they would be at," and had not a definite view of the end towards which effort should be directed.

In the pre-scientific days the end which men of affairs kept in view, when debating economic affairs, was clearly understood; the political power of the realm was the object they put before them, and they considered the various elements—sea-power, shipping, food supply, industry—which were necessary factors in creating and maintaining the power of Great Britain. Measures were regarded as expedient or in-expedient, according as it appeared that they would or would not promote this aim. Adam Smith, despite all the changes which he introduced into the study, still retained this habit of thought. He definitely accepted the principle that "Defence is of much more importance than Opulence[1]."

During the last five and twenty years it may be said that the public has come to recognise a very different aim as well worth attending to. We are not so much concerned at the present time about the power of the country as about the welfare of the inhabitants. We recognise that the defence of the realm is essential to welfare, but we are no longer so much concerned about building up the power of the country, or so ready to engage in aggressive wars for the sake of commercial advantage, as Englishmen were in the eighteenth century. Still less are we satisfied with Opulence and the mere accumulation of material goods ; it is a common place that we desire to promote the well-being of the inhabitants, physical, moral and intellectual. There are sure to be diverse views at different times as to the elements of Welfare, which it is best worth while trying to secure, and the means of obtaining them ; but we should all be agreed in viewing critically any tendencies which were inimical to Welfare, even if they undoubtedly make for an advance in Opulence. Such elements of Welfare, as security and health, are advantageous to the community generally, but no individual can purchase them for himself; they lie outside the columns of the ledger. Welfare cannot be obtained in definite quantities by paying for it ; but, on the other hand, it cannot be secured without

[1] *Wealth of Nations*, IV. ii. p. 188.

cost; it involves the sacrifice of some wealth in the present, whatever the final compensation may be. The advantage to any single individual from a public boon—improved government or better conditions for health and education—is very difficult to assess; and the individuals who contribute most, will rarely, if ever, be those who reap the greatest benefit personally. The public good and common Welfare are objects towards which men are compelled to contribute according to the means they possess, rather than according to the benefits they are likely to receive. It is on these general lines that we are trying to make progress.

The Classical Economists had no such definite conception of an object towards which it was worth while to direct public effort. They had abandoned the pursuit of Power, as unnecessary, if it were not misdirected energy; and they were inclined to be satisfied with aiming at Opulence,—an increase of material wealth. They would not of course have said that Opulence was the one thing worth aiming at, and that material wealth was to be preferred to good government, just laws and cultured life. But they held that, in an ordinary way, Opulence gave the material means and opportunity for procuring these higher goods, and that by pursuing the path which afforded the largest mass of material wealth, we should have the greatest possibilities of Welfare within our reach. It was in this fashion that they were inclined to treat Opulence—material wealth— as the supreme consideration, and to view with sus-

picion all proposals for social improvement which
involved any interference with cheap production.
They feared that any diminution of wealth would
necessarily cause diminished Welfare. The Classical
Economists concentrated their attention on national
Opulence ; they saw the probable expense which came
from such measures as the Factory Acts, but they
could not see that some sacrifice of material wealth
might be rightly made, in the hope of securing a
greater degree of Welfare.

The Classical Economists were prevented from
attempting to weigh any proposed sacrifice of wealth
against prospective Welfare, because of their in-
adequate conception of national Opulence. They
regarded the wealth of the nation as the aggregate
of the possessions of individual citizens ; and hence
they came to hold that that which makes for the
increase of individual wealth, makes for the Opulence
of the realm as a whole. *Laissez faire,* as the system
which gives the greatest freedom for individual
enterprise, came to be regarded as the chief condition for increasing national Opulence ; and any
interference with *laissez faire* seemed likely to be
an injury to the community. This identification of
individual wealth with national resources is un-
satisfactory in various ways, but one of these is
obvious ; in concentrating thought on the aggregate
of individual wealth, men give attention to the
accumulations of the past and the activities of the
present ; this standpoint does not lead them directly
to examine the possibilities of the future. Maxims

which direct us how to make the most of what we actually have, with regard to existing conditions, may not be the wisest for developing our resources, material and human, with a view to the prosperity of future generations. A prudent regard to the material wealth of posterity may involve the sacrifice of wealth in the present by many individuals. Maxims based on *laissez faire* conceptions of Opulence are likely to be short-sighted, and there is a serious danger that they should be narrow. Events have shown that the philanthropists, and not the Classical Economists, were right in regard to the factory acts, even so far as Opulence is concerned. The philanthropists were striving to promote Welfare even at the sacrifice of wealth, but the Welfare has been attained, and wealth has been added thereto. Shortened hours have been compatible with improved efficiency; a genuine gain in human Welfare is quite likely to bring about a positive increase of material possessions.

In so far as they attempted to give advice on practical matters, the Classical Economists failed, because they temporarily forgot that their science was abstract. The theoretical principles which hold good, on certain assumptions and under definite limitations, cannot be transformed, ready made, into abstract maxims of practice which hold good universally. Their arguments called forth the indignant protest of Lord John Russell, as a man of affairs. " Wealth is the only object of their speculation ; nor do they much consider the two or three millions of people who may be reduced to utter beggary

in the course of their operations. This they call
diverting capital into another channel. Their reason-
ings lie so much in abstract terms, their speculations
deal so much by the gross, that they have the same
insensibility about the sufferings of a people that
a general has respecting the loss of men wearied out
by his operations[1]." Mr Haldane recognises that
Ricardo went too far " in insisting on rigidly laying
down abstract maxims of practice without looking to
right or left[2]"; but the academic coterie of the
present day have not learned by experience. They
intervene to give us a warning on a matter of
practical politics, without having made clear to the
world what the practical object is which they would
have us pursue. It is only accidentally and in a
haphazard way, that we can discover their conception
of the end to be aimed at. Sometimes it seems to
be Opulence,—the aggregate of individual possessions
in this country, whether produced here, or obtained
by a sort of tribute from abroad. Sometimes they
seem to idealise fluidity—the condition under which
material progress has occurred—as if it were an end
in itself. They are ready to condemn the mistakes
which were made by the Classical Economists in
regard to the shortening of hours and other measures
of social improvement; but they have not really
advanced to a different standpoint. The Classical
Economists were admirable in the clearness with

[1] Huntingdon Letter 1822, quoted in *The Commercial Policy of
Pitt and Peel*, p. 26.

[2] *Economic Journal*, xv. 501.

which they carried on scientific enquiries, and in this the modern English Professors have deliberately refused to follow their lead. The defects of the Classical Writers came out in their mode of applying their principles; and the modern coterie have done nothing to establish a claim to respectful attention for any opinion they may hold on practical affairs. They are not in a position to supply clearly thought out and reasoned guidance in regard to any practical question.

III. Economic Science has not stood altogether still since the time of Ricardo, or even of Bagehot; by relying on the help which these great writers give, we can advance beyond the point they reached. For practical Political Economy the one great need at the moment is a clearer and more definite conception of the end which we have dimly and half-consciously been working towards during the last half century— National Welfare. When this can be thought out more definitely, a mass of economic experience will be available in the light of which the proper means for attaining the end may be suggested and criticised. But one thing is clear: those who recognise that Welfare is the object towards which it is worth while to direct the national energies, are sure to feel that it is an object which we must take some pains to attain in a greater degree, and that it will never come of itself, by mere *laissez faire*. The Classical Economists, who were content to make Opulence the aim of economic life, were justified in saying that each man, in struggling for his own greater riches, was also working for the increase of national Opulence, and that this object could be generally obtained almost mechanically. But with Welfare it is different; the gain to any single individual from a public boon, is very difficult to assess. In the eager competition of individuals with one another, public objects, of general good and for the common advantage, may be overlooked and forgotten. It is necessary that they should be consciously and deliberately taken in hand by public authority; and there must be some interference with private interests, favourable to some and unfavourable to others, when any effort is made for promoting the common weal. In so far as the national resources and the aggregate of individual wealth are distinct, it is desirable that public authority should occasionally interfere, even for the sake of Opulence, so that due regard may be had not only to the immediate present but to a distant future as well. But if we go further than this, and seriously adopt Welfare present and future as the object to be pursued, then we must absolutely discard the principle of *laissez faire*. We must recognise that it is the function of government— imperial, national and municipal—to promote Opulence and all the other elements which go to make up Welfare. It will not do to let things drift; they must be taken in hand, consciously and deliberately, and become a principal object of governmental care[1]. Those who complain that British

[1] The danger of lowering the tone of public life if the state shall seriously attend to economic affairs, may easily be exaggerated.

interests have suffered under successive governments during the last fifty years, may remember that during this very period the *laissez faire* school has been dominant, so that no effort has been made to think out what are the interests of the community as a whole, apart from those of individual citizens, or to consider on what issue it is worth while to take a stand.

More than this. If we are to have a scientific treatment of practical economic problems, we must have clear ideas ; but we must also try to keep as close as may be to actual life and be ready to learn from experience. The academic coterie are too much absorbed in the analysis and measuring of motives to be prepared to deal with this aspect of affairs ; but the Historical School of Political Economy is thoroughly empirical. It looks to history to supply recorded observations as to the influences that have made for the progress of human societies or the reverse, during long periods of time and in many different lands ; by its help we can verify our conclusions as to whether some projected course is wise or not. Mr Haldane fully recognises the service which has been done and can be done by this School of economists in meeting the want which the Classical School failed to supply. "Each country must be profoundly affected by its

I doubt whether there is any real ground for fear as the chief causes of political corruption seem to me to be quite different (see my *Tariff Reform and Political Morality* in *Compatriot Club Lectures*, p. 302). But even if the danger is real we shall do better to face it, and so learn by experience how to deal with it, than to continue to let things drift.

economic policy, by its history, by the nature of the institutions which have grown up in it, by strategetic conditions such as those which affect a military nation like Germany, by its geographical position, and by a multitude of minor circumstances of which states-men must take account, and of which economists must take note before drawing practical conclusions." The Historical School of economists do not aim at formulating maxims of universal validity in regard to the action of all individuals[1]. Such universal principles would be barren, and might soon seem to be mere truisms; there is not much advantage in formulating the principle that all men are mortal. The Historical School try to examine recorded experience from all times and places as to the causes of the wealth of nations. The results they obtain in the study of any one particular nation are likely to have a practical value to the statesmen of that nation, and may even be of some help in arguing by analogy as to the course which should be pursued or

---

[1] Dr Aubry states very clearly the line which is taken by Bastiat and analytical Economists generally in regard to the importance of History. They do not treat it as recording experience from which we can learn about the actual development of human affairs, but merely as supplying vivid illustrations of universal principles. They claim to possess in economic science, the knowledge of "irresistible, economic laws of nature." "If we find pleasure," he writes, "in making investigations into the past of a people it is to give precision and confirmation to the rational verities which the examination of existing phenomena has enabled us to obtain." (*Étude critique de la politique commerciale de l'Angleterre à l'égard de ses Colonies*, p. 185.) The *Spectator* particularly commends this method of dealing with History to Free Traders. (5 Aug., 1905, p. 193 n.)

avoided by another nation. A careful study of our own immediate past may help us to decide on the direction in which it is best worth while to look for the next step in advance. Recorded experience as to the progress of our own and other peoples may furnish suggestions as to the different schemes which it is desirable to pursue in the effort to secure a greater measure of national Welfare in each of the various countries which make up the British Empire.

MR ST LOE STRACHEY

AND

IMPERIAL SENTIMENT.

The paradoxical character of Free Trade Imperialism.

I. The true Imperial Spirit contrasted with mere regard to British Interests.

II. The grievances of the colonies in the second quarter of the nineteenth century need not recur under organised colonial co-operation.

III. The fostering of Sentiment is insufficient, without the establishment of a common Understanding in regard to commercial intercourse.

IV. *Laissez faire* involves the sacrifice of Colonial Interests.

MR ST LOE STRACHEY

AND

IMPERIAL SENTIMENT.

TARIFF Reformers cannot but feel that they have a long and arduous campaign before them; and they will be able to conduct it more effectively, if they can make up their minds as to the key of the position they are attacking. So far as I can judge, I am inclined to think that the Free Trade Imperialists occupy this point of vantage. With the object of estimating its strength, we cannot do better than examine the opinions expressed, during his electoral campaign and in his published writings, by Mr St Loe Strachey. As editor of the *Spectator* he has been a very vigorous defender of our present fiscal arrangements; though an Englishman, he had the compliment paid him of being selected by Scotch University Free Traders as their champion. He may be regarded as a typical representative of the Free Trade Imperialists; and if it can be shown that the position which he takes is quite untenable, we may hope that public opinion will veer more decidedly in the direction of reform.

The sympathy is so strong, in spite of deep differences, between Fiscal Reformers and Free Trade Imperialists, that it is not easy to see at first where the line of cleavage really begins. The severance seems to me to be due to the difference in their views as to the functions of the State in regard to commerce. Our consideration of the manner in which practical economic questions may best be dealt with scientifically has led us to the conclusion that it is the function of the Imperial Government to attend to the increase of opulence and all other elements of welfare throughout the Empire. This was the conclusion which was forced upon us by a consideration of the best methods of apprehending economic ideas, and of applying economic experience. It is a fair statement of the position taken by Tariff Reformers; but the Free Trade Imperialists abjure this principle altogether. They protest that their enthusiasm for the Empire renders them jealous of any departure from the maxims of *laissez faire*. In his address to the graduates of the Universities of Edinburgh and St Andrews, Mr Strachey insisted that "the Empire is in truth the gift of Free Trade. Some sixty years ago," he said, "we had a system of preferential trade with the Colonies which, had it not been abandoned, would inevitably have destroyed the Empire. As soon as it had been abandoned, but not till then, did the true Imperial spirit begin to develop." In the essay he has contributed to Mr Goldmann's excellent book, *The Empire in the Twentieth Century*, Mr Strachey develops this thesis more fully and traces the genesis of an anti-colonial feeling to the grievances suffered by English merchants during the period when preferences were given by the Mother Country to some of the colonies. This began in 1807; but it was hardly adopted as a regular practice till 1822, so that we may take the second quarter of the nineteenth century as the time when it prevailed. "A very little reflection," Mr Strachey writes, "will show whence arose this unfavourable feeling towards the Colonies, which remember was specially strong in the commercial class, and was reflected from it into the minds of our statesmen. I believe it came from the system of Preference, which oppressed our trading and commercial classes at every turn....The Colonies were unpopular, and with those persons who declared that they would soon be independent, the wish was father to the thought. They longed to get rid of the burden of preferential trade and believed that it would only disappear with independence. Hence the men who belonged to, or who were brought up in, the preferential period tended to become Little Englanders[1]." Mr Strachey reiterates his conviction with such force that it cannot fail to be impressive. "The maxim 'No Free Trade no Empire' is no mere assertion of a personal opinion, but a statement which can be made good by an appeal to the teachings of history. It is a fact, not a theory[2]." But after all History does not teach anything at all to those who have no

[1] *The Empire in the Twentieth Century*, pp. 154, 155.
[2] *Ib.* 144.

mind to learn. Though Mr Strachey has strangely misread the story of the preferential period, his account of it is exactly what might be expected from anyone who only appeals to history for illustrations of his preconceived opinions[1].

Reserving the question as to whether Mr Strachey's opinion really rests on a solid basis of fact, we may note in passing that it is curiously paradoxical. Cobden and the Anti-Corn Law League had a thoroughly consistent scheme, politically and economically : they were definitely anti-Imperialist, and they advocated a *laissez faire* policy in things economic, because they regarded it as a means to the political end they had in view. "The Colonial System with all its dazzling appeals to the passions of the people can never be got rid of, except by the indirect process of Free Trade, which will gradually and imperceptibly loose the bands which unite our Colonies to us by a mistaken notion of self-interest[2]."

It was thus that Cobden wrote in 1842, and subsequently he became acquainted with Bastiat[3], who was fanatically anti-Imperialistic. This French enthusiast held that, since security for trade and intercourse was an interest which concerned all nations, there was no need for any one of them to be at pains to preserve and maintain it, and that consequently expenditure on political objects was

[1] See above, p. 30, note.
[2] Morley, *Life of Cobden*, I. 230.
[3] Compare Mr Welsford's article on *Cobden's Foreign Teacher* in the *National Review*, December, 1905.

mere waste; he failed to recognise the well-known principle that what is the common concern of many people is quite likely to be neglected altogether. Bastiat believed Free Trade was the means of destroying the political institutions he disliked, and Cobden shared his view : this was their chief reason for advocating it enthusiastically. But Mr Strachey and the Free Trade Imperialists assure us that they reject Cobden's political views absolutely; they are prepared to stigmatise the Little Englander, who would wish to see Canada annexed to the United States, as guilty of "treachery." It is only on the economic side that they follow Cobden; like him they advocate Free Trade, but curiously enough they advocate it for exactly the opposite reason to that which he put forward. Cobden believed that Free Trade would weaken the Empire, while Mr Strachey holds that it has strengthened it and that it is essential to its very existence. "The one thing that can and would ruin the Empire would be the abandonment of Free Trade, in any shape or form[1]." When we find them so closely associated with Little Englanders economically, we may feel that it is all the more necessary to examine whether their political anticipations are well-founded.

I. On the face of it, the view that "the true Imperial spirit only began to develop" after 1846 is quite absurd. From the very beginning of our colonial enterprise, three centuries ago, there have always been two parties in regard to colonisation

[1] *The Empire in the Twentieth Century*, p. 158.

and Empire, just as there are to-day. Some men
have regarded it as a duty for this country to use
its power and influence by fostering civilised life in
the most distant parts of the earth; while many
others have cared nothing for the Colonies, except in
so far as they subserved the material interests of this
country. The true Imperial spirit may be found,
long before the earliest attempt at colonisation was
made, in such a man as Sir Francis Drake, whom
Mr Corbett describes in his fascinating work as eager
to found an English Empire on the Pacific Coast of
North America[1]. In the actual attempts at colonisation in the time of Elizabeth and her Stuart successors
there is abundant evidence of this sense of duty[2];
the most casual reader cannot fail to recognise it in
the action of the Virginia Company, or in the pages
of such an author as Richard Hakluyt[3]. Sir William

[1] *Drake and the Tudor Navy*, p. 312. Drake's own words are
worth quoting: " Wherefore, in the name and to the use of her
most excellent maiesty, he tooke the scepter, crowne, and dignity
of the sayd countrie into his hand; wishing nothing more than
that it had layen so fitly for her maiesty to enjoy, as it was now
her proper owne, and that the riches and treasures thereof (where-
with in the upland countries it abounds) might with as great con-
ueniency be transported, to the enriching of her kingdome here at
home, as it is in plenty to be attained there; and especially that so
tractable and louing a people as they shewed themselves to be,
might haue meanes to have manifested their most willing obedience
the more unto her, and by her meanes, as a mother and nurse of
the Church of Christ, might by preaching of the Gospell be brought
to the right knowledge and obedience of the true and euerliving
God." Drake's *World Encompassed*, ed. W. S. W. Vaux, p. 129.

[2] See my *Growth of English Industry and Commerce in Modern
Times* (1903), p. 336.

[3] *Voyages*, III. 302.

Hunter and other recent writers regard it as one of the leading motives in Cromwell's policy, though as it seems to me on insufficient grounds[1]. At all events it finds ample expression[2] after the Restoration in the great era of English expansion, when Englishmen were really entering on their vast heritage; the East India Company secured their footing in Bombay, the Guinea Company in Africa, and the Hudson's Bay Company beyond Canada; the men who did these things had a magnificent sense of the destiny of England as a world-power. It is easy enough to trace the same sense of duty and responsibility all through the eighteenth century, but it may suffice to refer to the name of Chatham. Willingness to sacrifice something for the Colonies may be taken as the test of a sense of duty in regard to them, and of the recognition of our mission as a race in the world.

It is also true, however, that since the Colonies were first founded there have always been men who looked on them with jealousy, and who only cared about them in so far as they subserved English interests, in the narrowest sense of the word. During the seventeenth century it was a matter of common remark that Spain had been weakened by the effort to develop a colonial empire, and fears were expressed lest, in planting America, England should be drained of money, and of men who could be usefully employed at home. In

[1] On the *Imperialism of Cromwell*, see below, p. 106.

[2] Compare the official instructions to the Council for Foreign Plantations, Dec. 1, 1660. *Cal. State Papers Col.* 1574–1660, p. 492; also *Cal. State Papers Col.* 1669–1674, *A. and W. I.*, No. 225.

the eighteenth century Dr Tucker, the Dean of Gloucester, set the fashion of treating the retention of the Colonies as a mere question of profit and loss; and demonstrated that the political responsibilities they entailed were so costly that it was absurd to engage in colonisation at all. Before the preferential period began, Sir John Sinclair gave vehement expression to this view[1]: "The whole expenses we have been put to, in consequence of our possessing colonies on the continent of North America may be estimated at forty millions, in addition to the charges of at least two wars, which cost us above 240 millions more, and which were entered into principally on their account.

"It is the more necessary to bring forward inquiries into this branch of our expenditure, as the rage for colonization has not as yet been driven from the councils of this country. We have lost New England; but a New Wales has since started up. How many millions it may cost may be the subject of the calculations of succeeding financiers, a century hence, unless by the exertions of some able statesman that source of future waste and extravagance is prevented." In his case the anti-colonial opinion was based on financial and political grounds, and had no connection with the grievances which may have been felt by the commercial classes.

The same line of cleavage in regard to opinion can be easily traced all through the period to which

[1] *History of the Public Revenue of the British Empire*, 3rd edition, II. 101.

Mr Strachey has given special attention. Men who regarded the Colonies from the point of view of interest were of course prepared to fasten on any inconvenience which arose in connection with these possessions. The system of preferences was begun about 1807, during the Napoleonic War, when England was excluded from the Baltic and it became a matter of pressing importance to obtain a large supply of timber and naval stores from Canada[1]. It was deliberately maintained by Huskisson in 1822 in spite of the inconvenience which it caused to the shipping interests; but the extent of the grievance among the commercial classes may easily be exaggerated, and in any case it is absurd to suggest that the unfavourable feeling towards the Colonies was reflected from the commercial classes into the minds of our statesmen[2]. Political anti-Imperialism was a much older thing than the preferential tariffs, though perhaps too much stress may be laid on the occasional and petulant utterances of statesmen who found it difficult to see their way through some problem of Colonial politics. Even during this period, however, of indifference and neglect there was ample evidence of the true Imperial spirit and the sense of duty towards the Colonies. These come out clearly in the principles of Colonial government which were laid down by Mr Pitt in the Quebec Government Bill, and in the speeches of such men as Huskisson and Peel. The great mission of Lord Durham and the grant of

[1] Hills, *Colonial Preference*, in *Compatriot Club Lectures*, p. 285.
[2] *The Empire in the Twentieth Century*, p. 154.

responsible government to Canada were the most important step in the advance of the Colonies during the nineteenth century, and this occurred in 1840, during the preferential period. The active work of Wakefield and the Society for systematic colonisation was commenced during the same era : Mr Strachey ignores them altogether and asserts that "almost all the audible voices were raised against the continuance" of the Empire. At least the duty of Englishmen was not forgotten at one centre of sound learning and religious education. William Whewell, then a Fellow of Trinity, was a man of a truly Imperial spirit. "Our place among the isles of the ocean, our fair havens and lofty beacon-sites, our commerce and our fleets, our stores and treasures, are thus held by us as subjects and servants of the Governor of the Universe[1]. Nor is this all: our better and finer possessions, our advantages of character and mind, are no less held and exercised under His control and guidance ;—the endowments of the soul, courage and invention, energy and endurance ; the indomitable will, which no resistance of the elemental world can tame ; the heart which can brace the sinews under the fierce smiting of the tropical sun ; the eye which can look steadfastly, though the ice close round like a tomb, and life seem departing with departing light and warmth; the temper on which hope deferred acts only as a fresh stimulus to action ; the sagacity in governing distant lands, which is sharpened, not

---

[1] On *Religion and Political Life*, see below, p. 91.

baffled, by variety of circumstances. They are, we may venture to believe, the instruments of a good, which however it may begin with us, is to extend to the uttermost parts of the earth, and to the remotest ages." Such utterances during the period of preference need not be ignored. Nor am I able to agree with Mr Strachey in thinking that indifference to the Colonies has been entirely exorcised from the minds of the politicians who have been brought up since the Free Trade era opened. It is still true that those who are absorbed in the consideration of British interests, in a narrow and insular sense, are not prepared to make any sacrifice for the sake of maintaining the unity and influence of the Empire[1].

---

[1] The "pawkiness" which his contemporaries noticed in Sir John Sinclair is admirably illustrated by the attitude he took towards those who had suffered from their loyalty to this country during the American War. He preens himself on our liberality, while he is also anxious to guard against any mistaken expectations. "It must yield no small degree of satisfaction, to every citizen of this country, to be able to produce so unparalleled an instance of national liberality and spirit; and the business being now in some measure concluded, the most penurious can hardly wish it undone, notwithstanding the expensive consequences of which it has been productive. It is to be hoped, however, that some caution will be exercised for the future, in giving way to similar claims. It will not be difficult, if any other rebellion should arise in the foreign possessions of Great Britain, to practise a thousand frauds upon the public, if such a principle is to be adopted in future. The timid and the wealthy, under the pretence of loyalty, will naturally fly from the scene of war, and shelter themselves in a country, by which their property will be restored, if it proves successful, or who will recompense them for their losses, if otherwise. The leaders of the rebellion will engage with more spirit in the cause, from the hopes of confiscation and plunder; and enriched with the spoils of those who have fled, will undergo any

They appear to have little sympathy with the men who are bearing the white man's burden in distant places and in trying times. They are prepared to "wash their hands" of the difficulties in the Transvaal. The determination to grant responsible government without enquiry as to the conditions in which it will be carried on, and with no regard to the terrible injury which may be inflicted on men of British race, is suggestive of an anxiety to shirk a difficult task at all hazards. The true Imperial spirit of the present House of Commons does not appear to exercise much influence on the votes of the Free Traders.

In so far as the Colonies were aggrieved with the Mother Country during the second quarter of the nineteenth century, it was not primarily on economic grounds. There had been a complete change of policy since the breach with the American Colonies[1]. Till that time the economic activities of the Colonies had been deliberately controlled in the interest of the Mother Country, though they had had practical freedom to govern themselves in other matters ; there was little interference with their own internal affairs

---

extremity sooner than relinquish them: and thus Great Britain may subject itself to an enormous expense, for the purpose of rewarding the attachment of those, who never could be of any material service to it, whilst the war is rendered at the same time more difficult to make up, and more inveterate." It is always pleasant to contemplate our own generosity, especially if, like the Anti-Slavery philanthropists, we have the faculty of forgetting that it has been exercised at other people's expense.

[1] Sir C. Adderley (Lord Norton), *Review of "The Colonial Policy of Lord J. Russell's Administration," by Earl Grey*, p. 2.

till the passing of the Stamp Act. Whether well founded or not, an opinion had become current in England that the economic disabilities had been the main cause of the American Rebellion; and under Pitt's statesmanlike scheme of reconstruction every attempt was made to give the fullest economic advantages to Canada and the West Indian Colonies[1]. Another danger was uppermost in men's minds when the institutions of Canada were reorganised in 1792; two different races were living in that land; the Upper Province and the townships of the Lower Province were mostly inhabited by Englishmen, while the great majority of the population of the Lower Province consisted of Frenchmen, who had had very full rights as to their system of law and land tenure secured to them by the Treaty of Paris. It did not seem desirable to the statesmen of the day to create one assembly, in which these conflicting elements would struggle for the mastery; Pitt created two separate representative assemblies[2], one for each province, in the hope that they would express the views which each section took of their own interests. But the ministry believed that the good government of both races and security for the well-being of each, as well as the wise development of the resources of Canada as a whole, could be best exercised by the advisers of the Crown of Great Britain, who would have no personal interests, but could look dispassionately at

[1] See my *Rise and Decline of the Free Trade Movement*, p. 23.
[2] 31 Geo. III. c. 31.

the public good[1]. The scheme had many merits, perhaps it was the best possible scheme for the time ; the principle of Pitt's constitutional measures, unlike his project for commercial freedom, was generally accepted[2]. But the new system had one disastrous result ; it engendered in the Colonial Office a dangerous feeling of moral superiority. The administrators at home came to regard themselves as the guardians of public virtue and to suspect the Colonists of urging a narrow and short-sighted policy. The deep philanthropic feeling which was stirred in this country in regard to the slave trade, and later in regard to the treatment of native races[3], told in the same direction ; while the conflicts between the great trading Companies, who carried on operations in Canada, demanded the attention of the home government to their injudicious treatment of public resources. As a result there was much interference, of an irritating sort,—and not less irritating because it was ill-informed—in regard to internal affairs of many kinds, which had been left to the Colonists themselves in the period before 1776. Ecclesiastical

---

[1] "If the Lower Province were to oppose the Upper, by imposing exorbitant duties, it was competent to this country to hold the balance between the two provinces and to remove the grievance. Lord Granville." *Parl. Hist.*, XXIX. 657.

[2] Canadian opinion was not unanimous in condemning this form of government at the time it was discarded. William Dunlop, of Gairbraid, the pioneer in the Huron Tract, was anxious to maintain the old system ; he believed that the settlers had better conditions under the Crown than they could hope to enjoy under responsible government in the Colony.

[3] *Reports* 1837, VII.

questions in Canada[1], labour questions in the West Indies[2], and land questions in South Africa and Australia, gave rise to considerable irritation. As compared with these, the grievances caused by the injudicious granting of preferences was quite unimportant; it is probably true that the Canadian timber trade was stimulated in a way that was detrimental to the steady development of the Colony[3]; but there can be no doubt that very general disappointment was felt when the system of preferences—especially the preference of corn—was brought to an end, without much consideration for the effects on the Colony and merely as an incident in the change of economic policy adopted by the Mother Country[4]. The supercilious interference in their internal affairs, which was alleged to be necessary on moral grounds and which recurred during this period, was a real grievance.

[1] *Reports* 1828, VII. 377, also Ap. 14.

[2] The West Indies were suffering from a shortage of labour after the importation of slaves from Africa was prohibited. The House of Commons appointed a Committee to consider the introduction of Chinese labour. They agreed, "(1) that there prevails amongst the male population of China a great disposition to emigrate, but that they almost universally emigrate with the intention of returning to their own country, and that a considerable number do actually return. (2) That the Chinese emigrants have uniformly conducted themselves with the greatest propriety and order, and have been peculiarly instrumental in promoting the improvement of those countries to which they have emigrated." (*Reports* 1810–11, II. 409.) The Committee saw no means of suggesting a scheme that would be likely to meet the views of the Chinese Government, and did not make any proposal.

[3] J. Davidson. *Commercial Federation and Colonial Trade Policy*, p. 49.

[4] *Ib.* 48.

The Colonists were convinced that they had more knowledge of the circumstances than officials at home; and many of them welcomed the establishment of responsible government because the Crown thereby publicly recognised that they were to be trusted to govern themselves.

In treating the commercial preferences as the primary cause of trouble between the Mother Country and the Colonies, Mr Strachey appears to me to be entirely mistaken; but even if his interpretation of history were correct it would be irrelevant to the matter in hand. No one proposes to reintroduce the old preferential system; we wish to introduce one that is new and essentially different from that which was definitely abandoned in 1846[1]. In the earlier half of the nineteenth century there was one self-governing nation in the United Kingdom of Great Britain and Ireland; the Colonies were mere dependencies and were treated as such both politically and economically. There are now five great self-governing nations in the British Empire, and no system of preferential trade can be thought of for a moment which does not take full account of the claims and aspirations of Colonial patriotism. There is no proposal that there should be any sort of coercion in the matter;

[1] 9 and 10 Victoria, c. 94. The question of principle was settled at this time. The discussions on the political significance of the change are interesting. See for example Lord Stanley's speech in the House of Lords, 1 July, 1847. 3 *Hansard*, xciii. 1086. A convenient statement of the rates of preference allowed for Colonial corn, sugar and timber, from 1823 to 1864, will be found in the Appendices to the *Return of Differential Duties, Reports* 1905, lxxii. 421–437.

in the present day, we in Great Britain have not the power thus to deflect the development of a Colony because of the requirements of the Mother Country, but we would not do it if we could. It is for the Canadians to consider for themselves what are the lines on which the prosperity of the great Dominion may be most wisely pursued. We have no wish to thwart them, or tie them to any economic principle we may lay down for ourselves. We fully recognise that they know their own interest best; and we believe that in whatever manner the resources of that great nation are most wisely developed, they will tend to the strength and security of the British Empire. Some of us have been able to learn by experience, and we do not propose to go back to anything that has been already condemned by the logic of events. The old Mercantile System, which governed our relations with our Colonies before 1776, had regard primarily to the maintenance of the resources and political power of Great Britain; any new system must be based on the common action of a confederation of nations freely co-operating for the welfare of the Empire as a whole. We Tariff Reformers are anxious to avoid the serious mistakes that were made during the earlier half of last century; we do not pretend to any superior wisdom which would justify us in dictating an economic policy to the Colonies, nor do we pretend that the men who go out to new countries necessarily live and move on a lower moral plane than that of the democracy at home. We are eagerly anxious that the Colonies should not in future suffer either injury or insult at our hands.

The lines on which the co-operation of the Colonial nations and the United Kingdom for the prosperity of all may best proceed, are at least suggested for us by recent developments of economic life. We must take account of experience in the past, but it is also desirable to be guided by the actual occurrences of our own day. America is the most rapidly progressive of all countries at the present time; and the trend of events there in business circles is at least suggestive of the course we must pursue if our affairs are to be managed on up-to-date principles. We have no desire to take a reactionary course and go back to the systems that served in the Middle Ages or in the eighteenth century. In the present day the great trading firms in the States recognise the extraordinary waste which occurs through keen competition[1],—waste which is injurious to producers and costly to consumers; they believe that all parties gain by coming into one organisation, in which producers of raw materials and commercial carriers and manufacturers combine for mutual benefit. That there are social and political difficulties connected with the Trusts I do not forget; they may pursue the wealth of the great corporations and their dependents, to the detriment of individuals. It may be most desirable to overhaul their action within the United States for the sake of public welfare; but I am looking at them economically; and economically

[1] J. W. Jenks, *The Trust Problem*, p. 21.

they appear to be a success, since their critics find it
so difficult to confine their operations and to put
them down. In their economic success they furnish
an example of the policy which our various political
communities might adopt with a view to securing the
prosperity of the Empire as a whole and in all its
parts. The characteristic feature of the Trusts—in
all their forms—is that they have discovered that in
the most modern and advanced industries, organisation can succeed better than mere competition. We
ought to consider seriously whether there are not
dangers in inter-racial competition, and risks in international competition; Free Traders regard these
things as the ideal economic condition with which
we dare not tamper at our peril. Personally I believe
that inter-racial competition is inconsistent with the
welfare both of the higher and the lower races, and
that it is desirable to get rid of the wastes of competition by organisation. The Trusts have shown that
it is possible to succeed economically on these lines.
Just as the railway companies, and the producers of
raw material and the manufacturers can each gain—
without appreciable public loss—by doing away with
the wastes of competition and entering into one
Trust—so I believe that every member of the British
Empire may gain by agreeing, consciously and
habitually, to co-operate with the others. We at home
have just what the Colonies lack, as Mr Wakefield
insisted early in last century[1]. Under their pro-

---

[1] *The Art of Colonisation.*

tective regulations we may secure a profitable field for the investment of capital in the development of industry within the Empire; we can, with careful selection from our superabundance, supply the elements of population which are needed to maintain a prosperous White Australia. Closer commercial relations between the different parts of the Empire are likely to bring about a healthy re-action on the appropriate industry of each. We need to have a well-considered economic policy for the whole Empire, which each self-governing portion is free to adopt, or to modify or to discard, in so far as it concerns itself.

There is a fundamental difference between the scheme of preferential arrangements now proposed and that which was in vogue in the first half of last century; but it is only by ignoring this fact that the Free Trade Imperialists are able to show any plausible reason for their fears. Their forecast as to the disastrous results which may be expected from commercial arrangements with the Colonies would be inept, even if the facts they allege were correct. As we have seen, however, it is quite a mistake to suppose that indifference to the Colonies politically had its origin in the scheme for maintaining close relations for trade, or that there is any ground for apprehending serious political danger if we shall make a new attempt in the same direction.

III. The Free Trade Imperialists are not to be trusted as intelligent interpreters of English Economic History, and it is difficult to feel confidence in them as exponents of political psychology. The *Spectator* has amassed large quantities of data for the study of animal intelligence, but this may not be the best preparation for appreciating the motives that weigh with English citizens in the discharge of their political duties, or the conditions that are favourable to the growth of patriotic sentiments.

Mr Strachey seems to think that if we attend to material conditions, the appropriate sentiment can be generated with certainty ; just as the chemist by supplying the necessary material in his retort, can generate any gas he pleases. But moral and political sentiments are too delicate to submit to this mode of treatment. The bouquet of a fine claret defies the chemist's power of analysis, and it cannot be produced to order ; it is a great mistake to suppose that we can generate sentiments at will from the economic conditions we devise. We now know it is a mistake, since the thing has been so often tried, without success. The Tories in the eighteenth century believed that by keeping the American Colonies in a state of dependence on this country for manufactured goods, they could generate a stronger sentiment of political loyalty—but they failed. The Cobdenites held that by setting an example of abandoning restrictions on trade, we could generate a cosmopolitan sentiment for Universal Peace and International Brotherhood—but they failed. Others argue that by encouraging colonial borrowing and increasing our investments in the Colonies, we may generate a sentiment of gratitude to this country [1]; much English capital has been invested at Johannesburg, but anyone who goes to South Africa will find that the capitalists have failed to generate a sentiment of gratitude. In the face of these notorious instances, do Free Traders really mean to assure us that by the mere neglect of the trading interests of the Empire we can strengthen the attachment of the Colonies?

This mistake as to the possibility of fostering sentiment is a defect in the scheme of Free Trade Imperialists, but the point is hardly worth much attention from those who think that it is possible to ascribe too much importance to sentiment in political life; such feeling is at best a means to an end, not the object we aim at. We wish to organise this Empire as a great and prosperous civilised polity, and mere sentiment does not offer a sufficient basis to build upon. It has its importance; the establishment of the *entente cordiale* between distinct political communities, such as England and France, has gone a long way to mollify any little irritation that may arise, and to disarm any possible hostility. This form of friendliness is appropriate to two countries that are and prefer to remain entirely distinct; its usefulness in such a case is due to the fact that it is mere sentiment, and does not commit either side to

---

[1] "No means so sure could be found of popularising in the Colonies the connection with the Mother Country as that of giving them the direct advantage of cheaper money." Sir C. W. Dilke, *Problems of Greater Britain*, II. 470.

overt action. But a more solid tie than sentiment is required between the different parts of one United Empire; there have been Military Empires and Commercial Empires, but it is difficult even to conceive a Sentimental Empire. We should beware of the danger of exaggerating the importance of sentiment, even though we do not disparage it in any way or forget that it is a cohesive force. We have all heard about the wise man who said that if he made the songs of the people he did not care who devised their laws. In our own day Mr Rudyard Kipling has exercised an incalculable influence by expressing the sentiment that had taken silent possession of the hearts of thousands of our fellow-citizens both here and across the seas. But sentiment is not even the main thing, and it is certainly not the sole thing. On Mafeking night in London there was abundant sign of sentiment, but it did not give the bystander an impression of real grit. Even though Mr St Loe Strachey should himself consent to write Imperialist lyrics for the music halls, we would not feel satisfied to dispense with all efforts in favour of binding the Empire together by other means.

If a closer union with the Colonies is to be brought about, it must appeal not to mere feeling, but to intelligence as well; not only to the hearts of the citizens of this Empire, but also to their brains. The people are bound together as members of a common stock, by the possession of a common tradition of free institutions, and public control of the

administration, and by common loyalty to the Crown;
there will be an immense strengthening of the union
if they are also united in cherishing the same policy
in common and putting it into practice. There are
many points where old countries and new differ
greatly; we cannot pursue the same policy in regard
to such internal affairs as education or railway
management or alcoholic drinks; but we may adopt
the same policy in regard to intercommunication
between different parts of the Empire; we can do it,
if we will. Farther, we know that in adopting this
course we would not be trusting to any speculation as
to probable results, but following proved experience.
Where separate political communities have adopted
a common commercial policy, closer cohesion for all
other purposes has been brought about. There are
two striking instances; the cases of our great industrial rivals America and Germany are conclusive.
At the close of the War of Independence the separate
States had hardly any effective ties of connection;
there were jealousies of many kinds which tended to
keep them apart, and they were held together by the
very loosest confederation. It was not till Alexander
Hamilton carried through the new constitution and
the whole area became one for commercial purposes[1],
that there was any sign of cohesion. Since his time
the course of events led the separate States to draw
more closely together, till as a result of the Civil
War, the Union triumphed and the whole has been
consolidated into one great nation. In Germany the

[1] F. S. Oliver, *Alexander Hamilton*, p. 141.

process has been more recent, but equally effective. Prussia used her hegemony to bring the other states of Germany into commercial union; and what were severed communities have been welded into a great military and industrial Empire. Nor is it only in states which have a continuous territory that this policy proves effective; the wisdom of the protective policy of France may be questioned in regard to many matters—for example its effect on shipping; but the increase of trade that has accrued under the new Colonial scheme is most striking[1]. No verbiage can explain away the force which rightly attaches to such examples.

We have then good grounds for hoping that a Colonial Conference would at least produce such mutual understanding that the main features of a common commercial policy might be shaped out; in so far as this was done, it would be possible for each of the five nations to consider how far they could adopt it for themselves. So long as no such policy is even outlined, it is impossible to see in what ways the Colonies and the Mother Country can consciously co-operate, or to know what, in the common interest it would be well, so far as is practicable, to avoid. There is only one obstacle to any attempt to come to such an understanding; it rests with ourselves. The colonists are clear that it is the duty of the Imperial Government to attend to the increase of opulence and all other elements of welfare throughout

[1] Franke, *Der Ausbau des heutigen Schutzzollsystems in Frankreich*, p. 122.

the Empire, and they are anxious to discuss the
topic. But the Free Trade Imperialists say no;
they still adopt the insulting attitude of conscious
superiority which was so mischievous during the
earlier half of last century. All the superciliousness
of the Free Trader comes out in the refusal to go un-
fettered into a Colonial Conference. He knows that
the Colonies are protectionist, and lets it be seen
that he despises them as unenlightened; he holds
that the governments of such countries must necessarily be corrupt; and he refuses to discuss a common
commercial policy with their statesmen. He is offen-
sively neglectful of the ancient maxim of constructive
statesmanship, that what concerns all should be considered by all.

IV. The attitude of Free Traders at this time,
whether they profess to be Imperialists or not, is a
serious danger to the Empire, not merely because it
subjects the Colonies to actual insult, but because it
is a constant menace of possible injury. So long as
we persist in our *laissez faire* policy there is no saying
how completely Colonial interests may be sacrificed
in arbitration with slim antagonists. Those who are
concerned with insular interests only, will always be
glad to advocate a peace at any price policy in the
House of Commons, since England will enjoy the
peace, and the Canadians or South Africans will have
to pay the price. For this reason, Tariff Reform is
the most important of all Imperial issues, on which
all else depends, since Great Britain can never be
expected to attempt to understand, or to make any

effort to protect the real interests of any one of her Colonies, till she abandons her present attitude of mind. The weakness of *laissez faire* Economics has been pointed out; it does not formulate any national end as distinct from the interests of particular citizens. So long as we remain under its tutelage, we fail to recognise clearly and consciously that we have national interests of our own, or to try to discover what the national interests of any of our Colonies really are. For the last half-century we have suffered in every part of the globe because we have appeared to be so careless of national interests, and so ready to yield them. There has been no foreign Power that has not been able, by a little bluff, to get the better of us. It is important, for our own self-respect, that we should make up our minds what we care about; it is necessary that we should make clear to our neighbours what we will not stand. The want of purpose and firmness in our diplomacy has been largely due to the plain fact that we do not as a nation know our own mind. If we are conscious of our real interests and take our stand upon them, we shall so far recover our dignity, that other nations will be less likely to try it on, and see how far they can twist the lion's tail. More than this, it is only as we show ourselves capable of appreciating and defending our own interests, that the Colonials will feel that their interests are safe in our care. The fiasco, when we meekly consented to arbitrate about the Alabama claims, without insisting on compensation for the Fenian raid in Canada[1], must not be permitted to recur.

[1] J. Pope, *Sir J. A. Macdonald*, II. 85—140.

The Colonies have no longer any cause to complain of our consciously subordinating their economic
interests to those of the Mother Country either
directly or indirectly ; it is to be hoped that for the
future no partisans will be permitted to insult them
without an effective protest at home. They are
beginning to be world-powers, with a claim for consideration in any agreements that may be made by
Great Britain with other world-powers. It will be an
evil day if the great Colonial nations begin to believe
that the Mother Country is so supine and careless
that her statesmen will not be at the trouble to try
to understand Colonial aims, or have fresh reason to
fear that we at home can never be trusted to maintain their interests in the world.

LORD ROSEBERY

AND

THE UNEMPLOYED.

Treating the question systematically.

I.   The origin of chronic unemployment through the disintegration of the national industrial system by the Industrial Revolution.

II.   The problem of unemployment cannot be separated from a consideration of the conditions of employment.

III. Does the remedy lie in increased disintegration or in reconstruction on a wider basis?

IV. The Open Door, kept open, and Large Production, as against Cheap Production and Free Trade.

LORD ROSEBERY

AND

THE UNEMPLOYED.

To many of us the chief attraction of Tariff Reform lies in its political aspects, and the prospect it offers of closer union with the Colonies. But this scheme for organising commercial intercourse throughout the Empire also appeals to those who are deeply concerned about social difficulties at home. The existence of large numbers of unemployed artisans and labourers, during a period when trade is fairly prosperous, calls for serious reflection. While on his tour in Cornwall last autumn, Lord Rosebery chose this subject as the chief topic of his speech at Penzance[1]; he criticised the action of the Unionist Government, and took exception to the measure they had passed with respect to the unemployed. He insisted, and rightly, that this great problem must be dealt with *systematically*; though he appeared to be content to leave to others the duty of thinking out, as well as of carrying

[1] 22 Nov., 1905.

out, the best means for dealing thoroughly with what has become a chronic disease at the heart of the Empire. It is, of course, easy enough for anyone to devise a Utopia from his inner consciousness, and to suggest some scheme of society that might work if human nature were other than it is, or that would be practicable in a less congested country : but we cannot hope, by merely giving play to fancy in this fash:)n, to find a remedy that can be applied in the present condition of the country. If we are in earnest about the necessity of systematic treatment, we must endeavour to form an opinion as to the circumstances which have given rise to this malady ; and taking account of the phase of economic development we have reached, we must try to get a clear idea of the means by which we may hope to obtain a gradual, but permanent cure.

I. Want of employment, in particular trades at particular times and places, has occurred over and over again in English life ; but the existence of a class of labourers who are chronically unemployed, and are in consequence becoming less and less fit to be employed, is a very different matter. There was indeed one period when the country was suffering from this evil very generally; in the latter half of the sixteenth century there appears to have been more serious difficulty from this cause than there is at the present time. The industrial organisation of the towns, in gilds and companies, had quite broken down ; while the increase of sheep farming, at the expense of tillage, led to a great reduction of the

scope for employment in rural districts. We need
not go back to such a distant era, however, as the
reign of Elizabeth for the cause of the present distress; under the dominance of the Mercantile System
there had been a reconstruction of society, in accord-
ance with the national economic policy and the
facilities for production which were available at the
time. It will suffice for our immediate purpose if we
turn our attention to the Industrial Revolution, which
occurred during the century between 1760 to 1860.
Writers who chronicle the course of material progress are fain to enumerate the extraordinary changes
in *things* which took place at this time,—the miles
of canals and railways which were opened, the quantities of cotton yarn and pig iron which were produced
and exported, and so forth. We are more concerned
with the changes as they affected the *relations of
persons*; briefly, we may say that the Revolution, which
occurred during this era, brought about incidentally a
complete disintegration of the existing social system.
It affected the stability of each man's position and
the security of his prospects, so that while it caused
an immense increase in the powers of production and
gave facilities for applying them in the most effective
fashion, it also tended to the formation of a class
of unemployed and unemployable. The matter was
summarised in anticipation by a writer who saw the
beginning of the changes which the Industrial Revolution so greatly accelerated; there has been a steady
" removing of multitudes of people from the natural
and fixed basis, land, to the artificial and fluctuating

basis, trade[1]." There is no prospect, even if it were desirable, that we can go back and reconstruct our society on the basis of a yeoman-cultivation of land; our business is to make the best of an industrial system which rests on the basis of trade.

A very few words may seem to bring out the extraordinary contrast between the eras before and after the Industrial Revolution. In 1760—the very time when the victories of Clive and Wolfe opened up extraordinary possibilities of commercial expansion—there seemed to be little scope for industrial progress. The great industries of the country were stagnating; the clothiers were at a loss for increased supplies of wool, and the exhaustion of our woods made it difficult to continue the smelting of iron. The revenue of the country showed no elasticity, and financiers were at their wits' end to devise new sources of taxation. The population was practically restricted, by the system in vogue for relieving the destitute, to the various localities in which it was settled; there was little opportunity and much discouragement to its redistribution from the less prosperous to the more progressive areas. The country was economically independent; the food supply obtained from native sources was steady and abundant; every man had a fair prospect of maintaining himself in comfort by his calling, though he had little prospect of obtaining great wealth. The working

[1] J. Massie, *Plan for the Establishment of Charity Houses*, p. 69, quoted in my *Growth of English Industry and Commerce in Modern Times*, p. 578.

classes suffered comparatively little from any fluctuations of trade; for many of them had small farms or agricultural occupations as by-employments, which furnished a subsidiary source of income. The apprenticeship system was firmly established in most of the industries of the country; but, however sharp a man might be in picking up the technique of a new calling, he had no legal right to practise a trade to which he had not been apprenticed. There was a maximum of *stability* under a very complete system of national regulation, but the social conditions were incompatible with rapid change and progress.

Under the influence of increasing commerce, and through the successful exercise of ingenuity, this stable social system was strained, and then broke down. The application of coal to the smelting and working of iron, the introduction of the flying-shuttle and of spinning machinery, could not be stopped or restrained; indeed there is no reason to suppose that any serious effort was made to restrict these inventions, till after they had been well established. In one way or another they all tended to bring about migration, and to interfere with the stable national system which had had its basis in the land. The iron trade started afresh and attracted labour to the regions where coal and iron were readily accessible; the woollen trade migrated to the West Riding, where the flying-shuttle had come most generally into use; the cotton trade developed by leaps and bounds in Lancashire and at some other centres. The social conditions, which were incompatible with economic progress, proved to be but feeble barriers ; they were easily swept away, and the Industrial Revolution was allowed to have free course.

The gain, and the incidental loss, may be most easily brought out if we now turn to 1860, and see the extraordinary contrast in the condition and resources of the country. The material prosperity of the nation had increased enormously, but it was dependent, not so much on the state of agriculture, as on the state of trade ; this had come to be the dominating interest in the economic life of the nation. The success with which Great Britain had borne the strain of the Napoleonic Wars, and of the depression that followed them, affords the best measure of the resources of the realm. The improved land management of the latter part of the eighteenth century had facilitated the provisioning of our ships ; the trade which we carried on, and the navy which protected it, gave us the means of foiling the designs of Bonaparte and maintaining effective resistance to his military despotism. In spite of the pressure of the debt, which had been incurred in connection with these exertions, a readjustment of taxation had been begun by Huskisson and Peel, and this had given elasticity to commerce ; while under the influence of the gold discoveries, the new facilities for communication, and the greater freedom of intercourse, the trade of the country increased enormously during the decade from 1850 to 1860.

Even more striking than the increase of national wealth had been the extraordinary expansion of Great

Britain in the era between 1760 and 1860. The victories of Clive and Wolfe had set us free from the danger of French attack either in India or Canada; we had already made good our footing then, but that was all. A century later, in 1860, British customs and traditions and society had begun to reproduce themselves in all quarters of the globe. The great branch of the Anglo-Saxon stock, which had broken off from the British Crown, was entering on the struggle from which the United States emerged as a consolidated nation; Canada had successfully passed through most of her troubles, and the last shred of tutelage was being withdrawn; with her experience and possibilities, she amply compensated for the loss the Empire had sustained when the thirteen Colonies made good their independence. Antipodean lands which had not been occupied in 1760 were being rapidly developed; in Australia and New Zealand the foundations of great communities of white men were being laid. In South Africa there were fair prospects—too soon to be overshadowed—of a great confederation under the British flag; while this country had obtained a more direct hold upon India and was organising a better administration. The vast emigration involved in this expansion would not have been possible so long as the vestiges of the old system remained. The Industrial Revolution by disintegrating society had introduced the fluidity of labour; and this had rendered it possible to establish a great Empire, which introduced and developed the traditions of the English race in every part of the world. This growth in the area of our Empire could, so far as I see, have never taken place unless the Industrial Revolution had loosened the fabric of society at home, and thus given scope for emigration abroad[1].

So far as the condition of individuals within the nation is concerned, the case is not so clear. Although an enormous growth in national wealth and a striking development of the territories under the authority of the Crown occurred, it may be doubted whether there had been much improvement in the welfare of the home population. There is no real standard of comparison possible, so that we cannot say for certain; in 1860 the working classes had possibilities of travel and intellectual interest that were not open to their predecessors a century before, when the current views of life were more limited. In 1860 tea was no longer treated as an enervating luxury, and beer was ceasing to be absolutely indispensable. It is probable that the standard of comfort of the aristocracy of labour had risen considerably; the lowest level of existence was not in all probability lower, but there were doubtless a much larger number on this low level, and perhaps a larger proportion of the community.

If it is difficult to formulate any definite result as to the labourer's precise command over comforts, it is still more difficult to estimate the alteration in his social status. The workman's chance of obtaining

[1] G. R. Porter, *Progress of the Nation*, p. 128. It is a matter for great regret that such large numbers of these emigrants have settled outside the bounds of the British Empire.

practical independence and becoming a master was far smaller in 1860 than it had been a century before; he had also far less prospect of constancy of employment at the later date, and no real opportunity of supplementing his income from other sources. Under the new conditions of employment there was far less stability for the workman's life and for his home than there had been in the pre-revolutionary days.

II. The problem of the unemployed cannot be dealt with as an isolated fact; it is directly and necessarily connected with the conditions of employment. The Industrial Revolution, as it ran its course in England, introduced fundamental alterations in the terms and circumstances in which men carried on their work; incidentally, it has given rise to conditions which render us liable to the recurring formation of a class of unemployed; it therefore behoves us to be constantly alive to the danger, so as to be as much as possible forearmed. Unemployment is primarily due to the fluctuations of business; these are to some extent inevitable, but under modern conditions they occur on an unexampled scale. Our chief industries depend, both for their materials and their markets, on uninterrupted commerce with distant parts of the world, and they are liable to be disturbed by incidents in most remote regions. A war on the other side of the world may stimulate some kinds of manufacturing and render others unremunerative; the requirements of the Russian and Japanese armies gave an unexpected

stimulus to the demand for woollen goods. The
changes in the tariff imposed by a foreign country
may have most serious consequences; and the speculations of an American dealer recently created a
temporary cotton famine, and caused serious decrease of employment. The era of mechanical invention has also introduced elements of uncertainty
into the industries which cater for our own market
exclusively. Great building operations in any one
place—such as the erection of new laboratories in
Cambridge—draw masons, carpenters, bricklayers,
and others to the town. When the operations are
over there is likely to be, for many of them,
a period of inactivity before they can find new
opportunities of employment, and some of them can
only hope to do so by migrating to other parts of the
country. The slow building operations of the Middle
Ages did not involve such a concentration of many
men at a particular place for a few months, or such
rapid dispersion as is now frequent. Modern methods
have brought about an increase of fluctuation of employment in trades of every kind, and those who are
thrown out of work from time to time, in one trade
or another, form a quota of the great class of unemployed. Since our prosperity is based on a
fluctuating basis, we cannot get rid of all these
causes of uncertainty, but we may set ourselves to
minimise them by every practicable means.

There is also a steady decrease in the demand for
labour in many particular callings owing to the
introduction of mechanical processes. There are of

course cases where the application of machinery is not prejudicial to labourers generally, even if it deprives those, who have some specialised form of skill, of their livelihood. The railway system of the country gives a far larger field for employment of every sort than was open in the days of coaches and waggons. But in such trades as printing, where the new machines that are being introduced do not stimulate a greatly increased demand, the use of mechanical appliances may be brought about at the expense of the labourers, and as a substitute for their work ; in such cases it is probable enough that they are unable to recoup themselves in any way, and this is another side from which the army of the unemployed is recruited.

Besides these mechanical changes, it appears that the action which has been taken in recent years, to improve the position of workmen as a class has not tended altogether to improve the prospects of steady and long-continued employment. Measures which were intended to correct the evils of irregularity have to some extent aggravated them ; and far from giving greater security to the workmen generally, are said to operate to the disadvantage of all but the picked men. In so far as a high standard of minimum wages is being maintained, there is a greater danger than before that the men who are not quite up to the mark, and therefore do not earn the money, will not be employed at all. In so far as the risk of accident is thrown upon the employers, they may be more careful not to employ those who are careless of the risks they incur themselves or may bring on others.

The improvement of the labourer's position in these respects may be desirable, despite the disadvantage it entails; but we may note what its disadvantages are, and see that there is a danger of increasing the numbers of the unemployed. The less reliable men may be taken on at times of special pressure, but on the whole they constitute, along with those who are thrown out of work by the fluctuations of trade, an industrial reserve army of unemployed[1], who tend to become inefficient.

This is one of the most serious points in the whole problem; for it calls attention to the fact that an unemployed class is apt to perpetuate itself. Those who are accidentally thrown out, tend to become inefficient and unsuited for employment. The obvious remedy, for such fluctuations as occur in the building trades, would appear to lie in organising facilities for migration, such as existed, at all events on the Continent, in medieval times. But our national system as created under Elizabeth left no scope for migration; and the English tradition of dealing with the poor has positively discouraged the man who travels in search of employment. The casual ward or common lodging-house do not supply an atmosphere in which the man who is migrating in search of employment is helped to retain his self-respect.

---

[1] Compare the speech by Mr G. B. Barnes, M.P., on the Compensation to Workmen Bill. *Times*, 27 March, 1906. For fuller details see the *Report of the Departmental Committee on Injuries to Workmen, Reports* 1904, LXXXVIII. pp. 781–3.

Modern conditions of employment have given scope for the operation of a more serious cause of inefficiency on the part of able-bodied adults. Many of them have never been properly trained to any kind of trade; there is a large demand for boys as messengers and the like ; in these occupations they earn good wages as boys but are not on the way to earn good wages as men. By doing away with the apprenticeship system, we have allowed the population to assume that a trade can be picked up; and it is not easy to get English boys to give the time which is necessary to learn a trade, either in a technical school or by apprenticeship, when they have such frequent opportunities of earning money in undisciplinary occupations.

Broadly speaking, it seems that the disintegration of industrial society, with the frequent fluctuations of trade, and increase of an untrained and inefficient element in the population, are the chief reasons for the existence of a large class of unemployed. The problem is not isolated, but is closely connected with changes in the conditions of employment ; and this view is confirmed when we contrast a country where the Industrial Revolution ran a somewhat different course. In Germany the forces of economic progress were not allowed such free progress as they had in England. Prince Bismarck deliberately set himself to preserve the old organisations of domestic industry[1], and used them as the basis on which his new schemes for the benefit of the workmen rested.

[1] Poschinger, *Prinz Bismark als Volkswirth*, I. 5.

The preservation of the medieval companies presented an effective barrier to the sudden and sweeping changes which were effected in this country by the Industrial Revolution. It has not in all probability been an unmixed gain to Germany; there has not been the fluidity and social detachment which is a necessary condition for the emigration of different elements of population. The difficulties which have attended German Colonial enterprise are doubtless due to other causes as well, such as the lack of shipping and of facilities for intercourse which characterised that land from the sixteenth to the nineteenth century; in its internal affairs the country suffered much from wars, and progress was slow. There have of course been fluctuations in German industry, and some of them very serious, but there has not been the same danger of creating an unemployed and unemployable class. The reorganisation of society on national lines, with effective training, with facilities for migration and old-age pensions, was effected by Bismarck on the foundation which the surviving institutions of the medieval towns supplied. German industrial society has been successfully modernised and nationalised without being disintegrated: as we look at it we may feel that prevention is better than cure[1].

[1] The contrast as regards social disintegration between England and Scotland is worth taking into account, not so much with regard to the present day, as with reference to the period of the Industrial Revolution when the problem of English pauperism assumed overwhelming dimensions. The medieval organisation of industry, which had been swept away in England under the

III. When we once realise the circumstances
which have occasioned the existence and the recruiting
of a class of unemployed in this country in modern
times, we may see the inadequacy of the measures
proposed by Mr Balfour's Government. They attempted to deal with the question of the unemployed
apart from the conditions of employment ; any remedy
which ignores the causes of the mischief can be at
best a mere palliative ; and in regard to social distress
palliatives may often be specially dangerous.   That
which is intended to alleviate temporary distress is
apt to help to perpetuate the mischief by removing
some of the disabilities attached to unemployment.

But on the other hand the suggestions which
have been put forward by Free Traders are not particularly illuminating ; the Liberals, as Mr Haldane
declares, are lacking in ideas[1]. Some of them are
inclined to protest that nothing is seriously wrong ;
while others vary from a position of mere senti-
mentalism, to one of the sternest economic orthodoxy.
On the one hand we hear of the magic of property,

Tudors, continued to be a practical power north of the Tweed till
the middle of the nineteenth century.   It was not powerful
enough to resist or to survive the Industrial Revolution, but it had
sufficed along with the stringent practice in regard to poor relief,
to prevent the emergence on a large scale of the forms of pauperism
from which England suffered. Great pains had been taken when
capitalism was being introduced in the seventeenth century to use
it as a means of absorbing those who were out of work. A. Dunlop,
Treatise on the Laws of Scotland relative to the Poor, p. 15.

[1] *Address to University Liberal Association*, Edinburgh, 27 Jan.
1906.

and of the extraordinary results that might be obtained by re-creating a peasant proprietorship. It may be so; but the logic of events is against it; the yeomanry were unable to hold their own in ordinary farming during the eighteenth century, and there is little reason to suppose that they would have a better chance now. Further, this class has never shown itself, in Great Britain and Ireland, as very enterprising in adopting new systems of cultivation, or devising new methods of marketing goods. Experience tells against this proposal as merely reactionary. On the other hand, there are public men who seem to rely for a cure on an additional dose of the liquefier that has caused the mischief; the trouble is due to the disintegration of society, and they would find salvation in ultra-individualism. Their aim is to secure still greater fluidity, so that it may be possible for every individual to adapt himself to change as rapidly as possible. It is in this sense that education is advocated; a general technical education, it is said, will produce a broad and intelligent manner of looking at work, so that the man will be adaptable, and ready to take up new methods, or, when necessary, to throw himself into some other employment, if that in which he has been brought up declines. Whether it is really possible to devise any scheme of education, which would have the expected results, may be doubted; but it is apparent that if this could be done, it would at best be a palliative, not a cure. Fluidity is a necessary condition for rapid progress, but it is not an ideal to be pursued at all costs. Mill recognised that a stationary state might be preferable to ruthless progress ; if society were reduced to a mere flux, it would be of doubtful advantage, so far as the further increase of wealth is concerned ; and it would certainly be incompatible, according to all experience, with a high degree of Welfare. The institution of the family cannot flourish unless there is a certain amount of stability ; the disintegration of the home has been a very serious symptom of the last half-century ; and any movement which went farther in this direction could not but aggravate the evil. There is more need to correct the excessive fluidity which at present exists, than to accelerate the very influences which have brought this distress upon us.

Serious as the case undoubtedly is, we need not regard it as hopeless, when we remember with what success a similar problem—indeed relatively to the times, a much more difficult problem—was dealt with in Elizabethan England. The reigns of Edward VI and Mary were marked by a terrible state of social disintegration. The medieval organisation of labour, in gilds for each town, had been working badly and had completely broken down ; while the changes in the management and in the ownership of land had caused the utmost disorder in the rural districts. Under these circumstances the Government attempted the Herculean task of reorganising English industrial society on a wider basis. The municipality was no longer to be treated as the unit for this purpose, but the conditions and requirements of the country as a whole were taken into account. The Justices of the Peace and other local authorities were the agents through which the Council obtained information, and also the agents by whom regulation was put into effect. The supply of corn available was supervised, not in the interests of particular towns, but with a view to the needs of the country as a whole. Arrangements for the training of skilled labour and the regulation of the terms of employment, both rural and urban, were dealt with in the same spirit. Great efforts were made to develop the maritime resources of the realm in all directions, and care was taken for the relief of the poor throughout all districts alike. So carefully was this scheme planned, and so persistently was it put into effect, that, as far as we can judge at this distance of time, the problems of pauperism, and of the unemployed, were successfully dealt with; while the industry of the country, both urban and rural, prospered immensely. Something approaching a cure was found, not by going back and re-codifying an old system, but by going forward to a new one. Indeed, the life of many municipalities revived through the healthy re-action afforded under a system devised on national lines, and thus built on a broader and firmer basis. There seems to be no reason why a similar attempt should not be made again, if our social and industrial system were constructed, not now on national, but on Imperial lines. It is the function of the Imperial Government to take account of and promote the opulence and other elements of welfare throughout the whole British Empire, and in so far as this was accomplished it would re-act favourably on the mother country.

IV. Since the Industrial Revolution our prosperity has rested upon the fluctuating basis of trade; if we are to obtain any stability in the future we must accept that fact. We cannot hope to eliminate fluctuations altogether, but we may aim at rendering them as little injurious as may be, by securing an open door and large markets for our goods. Industrial organisation must always be framed with reference to the available markets; the industrial organisation of each separate medieval town in gilds was merely municipal, and was built up with reference to the demands in its own market-place and at the neighbouring fairs. The industrial organisation of Elizabeth's time was national, and was devised with reference to the internal wants of the country as a whole, and with regard to the trade which special companies carried on at the particular foreign ports where their factories were established. We have now commercial connections in all parts of the world, and it is by securing command of as large a trade as possible that we may obtain a sound basis for reconstructing our industrial system, and find good prospects of absorbing the unemployed.

The question then is, How can we secure and retain the command of the largest and best markets? Cobden and his followers believed that this could be done mechanically, by aiming at the cheapest possible production, and taking no farther heed of the matter, but leaving our goods to force their way into every part of the world. We now see that this policy has failed to answer the expectations which were formed of it[1]; and that we must take pains to secure and retain the command of our present markets, and especially of opportunities for the sale of goods which involve the employment of many labourers. We are not satisfied with a mere "consumptive importing trade[2]," but hope to obtain a healthy re-action on home industry from extended foreign trade. It is all the more necessary that we should try to keep our footing with regard to such markets as those in the Colonies, which are rapidly growing.

In the middle ages and era of municipal economy, as well as under the Elizabethan System of national economy, the method of securing the command of the market was very simple; protection was applied in the strictest possible way so as to secure the home market; this is the foundation of the national policy which is in vogue both in Germany and the United States, where the principal object of policy is the exclusive possession of the home market. Doubtless in many parts of the British Empire this policy is still the best, and it has been adopted by most of our Colonies. Mill's argument as regards infant in-

[1] See my *Rise and Decline of the Free Trade Movement*, pp. 66, 87.

[2] *Britannia Languens* (1680), p. 126. The discussion in this book of the favourable or unfavourable influence which foreign trade may exercise upon the prosperity of a country internally is very interesting, and has a close bearing on the present conditions of English trade. The form of the author's argument is affected by the fact that the importation of silver from the New World had been such a stimulus to industry and that this had been brought in the course of trade.

dustries seems to me quite sound, and I believe that
for young and growing countries it is desirable to do
their best to obtain an exclusive market, if they are
really to develop the industries for which they are
suited. Even in the very different circumstances of the
United Kingdom there may be exceptional cases in
which it is desirable to obtain an exclusive market.
If anyone were to argue that in the present condition
of rural England it was worth while to provide an
exclusive market for fruit grown in the open air, and
to tax or prohibit the importation of plums, pears,
and cherries, there does not seem to be any very
serious objection.

So far as the great industries of this country are
concerned, however, we have outgrown that policy;
we cannot be satisfied with exclusive possession of
some markets, we require to command access to the
largest possible markets. The country's great fund
of wealth no longer consists in landed property, it
arises from trade; and for purposes of trade, we want
to find ourselves admitted to a large and increasing
market. An exclusive market must almost necessarily
be a limited if not a narrow one—controlled by a political authority in certain interests; access to large
and growing markets need be in no sense restricted or
confined. It is the policy which is most favourable
to industry; in old days, the industry of each town
was carefully regulated with reference to the known
market afforded by the town; the export trade of the
country was carefully limited with reference to the
official forecasts of the companies who were responsible

for conducting the business at particular factories. In modern times trade is to be pushed as far as may be, and access to as large markets as possible is the fundamental condition of industrial well-being. At present we are being driven out of our own home market by having goods dumped upon us, at rates at which they cannot be remuneratively manufactured anywhere in the world. There is no desire to have exclusive command of the home market, but there is a demand that that market shall not be gratuitously spoiled. We hold that freedom to retaliate would give us the best means of opposing the chronic dumping, which is a real evil.

Similarly, we do not ask for an exclusive market in the Colonies, or desire to sacrifice their development to the maintenance of British industries; but we hold that by a system of preferences, grounded on the sense of common political tradition and destiny, the access to these large and growing markets may be preserved. Under existing conditions we are being driven from one market after another, and we want at all hazards to secure our footing in those which are best worth retaining. In this way the industry of this country, both as regards the sources of materials and the opportunities for sale, may be put on a firm foundation. To the cry of Free Trade we would rejoin with the policy of the Open Market; Free Trade has failed to give us an Open Market for our goods either at home or abroad; Tariff Reformers believe that we can obtain both one and the other by taking power to retaliate, and by preferential arrangements with the Colonies. They urge that we should use the means approved by experience for securing that large and growing trade, which Cobden's method no longer ensures. Voluntary agreement with the Colonies may be the means of preserving to us constant access to large markets, and regular supplies of the commodities we import from abroad. There is no excuse for alleging that this Imperial scheme is a return to the national protective policy which was in vogue in "the hungry forties." We recognise that mischief would result from attempting to get an exclusive market either for manufactures or ordinary produce at home—say from a 40/- instead of a 2/- duty on corn. We cannot admit that the same evils are likely to arise in connection with the very different policy we advocate of endeavouring to enlarge the opportunities for commercial intercourse. Our opponents complain that they cannot understand us, but even this is no adequate excuse for the misrepresentation involved in raising the cry of the little loaf.

We need not discuss the possibility of going back to the old days of municipal organisation, or national organisation ; we could not do it if we tried, since we have outgrown them both. But we may hope to create such Imperial organisation as will react on the conditions of employment in Great Britain, and therefore on the class of unemployed. Our industry depends on trade ; the broader the basis on which our trade is carried on, the firmer is the structure which rests upon it. The weakness of the policy of exclusive markets is that it means comparatively limited markets, and that fluctuations are likely to be more severe. The policy of the open door, and of access to large markets, offers the hope of compensation in one direction for losses in another, and gives the greatest prospect that there need be no sudden interruption or long-continued depression of an industry. These violent changes have been the principal occasion for throwing labourers out of work. The other causes of unemployment, in lack of training and vagrancy, must be dealt with apart from any special commercial policy; but the extent of our markets, and the industries which are most remunerative, must not be left out of account in considering what system it is practicable to adopt. The systematic improvement of the powers of labour and amelioration of its conditions can only be effected in such a country as the United Kingdom by the introduction of larger elements of stability into our social system.

More stability is needed, not only for labour but for capital. Security against ruinous competition and security for moderate returns are conditions which favour industrial enterprise; this we hope to increase by means of retaliation and preference, and the access to large markets, which can be preserved by agreement. Recent experience has taught us to reverse the favourite industrial maxim of the Classical Economists; they held that by aiming at cheapness a country could produce largely; while we have learned that large production is the thing to aim at, since production on a large scale, with good organisation, is necessarily cheap production. The time has gone by

when cheap food, low wages, and the "last hour"
were regarded as the foundations of our national
prosperity; the securing of large and growing markets,
by agreement, is compatible with favourable conditions for the employed, and offers a prospect of the
absorption of the unemployed and a gradual cure of
the evil. But the first step to be taken as a practical
thing is to enter into conference with the Colonies
and see what agreement it is possible for us to make
with them.

This course also offers the best prospect of introducing the most wholesome palliatives of the present
distress. The Colonies are rightly jealous of any
scheme which might lead to the large introduction of
undesirables, but they are eager to find room for men
and women of the right sort. There need be little
difficulty in arranging for the deportation of numbers
of the children, who would be only too likely to swell
the ranks of the unemployed in this country, but who
might be turned into useful members of society in
Colonial homes. Nor is the case of the adults hopeless; many men, though unskilled, might after being
subjected to the discipline of farm colonies, prove that
they were by no means wastrels, but that they would
be ready to do good work under new conditions.
With the help of our Colonies, and to their advantage, we may organise some immediate palliatives,
while we are also moving towards a radical cure.

It is interesting to see how a great idea persists
and fructifies; Mr E. G. Wakefield was the pioneer of
an Imperial Economic System; he showed how the

requirements of the various parts of the Empire fit into and supplement one another naturally; he aimed at encouraging the communication to which this interdependence lends itself, so as consciously to promote the growth of one great community, comprising separate self-governing nations in every part of the globe. The Free Traders, with their reliance on cheap production and their cosmopolitan sentiments, diverted attention from this scheme for a time[1]. We owe much to them, for we have learned not only all that they could teach, but much that they never knew as to the limits within which their principles hold good. We recognise the importance of the open door, but we have come to see that it will not stay open of itself, as they thought, but that it needs to be kept open. In the light of the vicissitudes of the last half-century and the changes in our own and other countries, the ideas which Mr Wakefield adumbrated, have assumed a more definite shape. The building up of a great Imperial polity to maintain and diffuse the noblest traditions of our race is a grand ideal ; we may hope to discover the means by which it can be realised, if we set ourselves to learn from experience.

[1] Seeley, *Expansion of England*, p. 73.

APPENDIX.

RELIGION AND POLITICAL LIFE[1].

THE Battle of Trafalgar is memorable in the history of Naval Warfare as an unprecedented victory; and it also marks an epoch in the history of the English people. The great aim, for which our statesmen had been striving for more than two centuries, was at last accomplished, since our navy had attained supremacy at sea. The achievement could not fail to have an effect on national life by modifying national ideals. From that day onwards the intensely bitter rivalry with our hereditary foes—France and Spain—began to be an anachronism; it is no longer regarded as essential for the patriotic Englishman "to hate a Frenchman as he does the devil[2]." This country could afford to be content with her success, and was no longer so anxious either to add to her resources or to humiliate her neighbours. Our political ambition was satisfied if we could maintain an apparently unassailable position, and this object could hardly inspire such ready self-sacrifice as had

[1] A sermon on Ps. cxxvii. 1, 2, preached before the University of Cambridge, 22 Oct., 1905, the Centenary of Trafalgar.

[2] Mahan, *Life of Nelson*, p. 86.

been shown in the struggle for supremacy. The change is very real; perhaps we can hardly yet say whether it is unwholesome, and is to be regarded as a sign of a loss of virility and of national decadence. British energy could henceforth be thrown more unreservedly into the paths of industry and commerce, and the Battle of Trafalgar opened up new directions in which this peaceful growth might extend. Whatever unrest and complication there might be in continental politics, Great Britain was free to pursue her destiny in all the distant regions to which she had recourse. Hitherto her Colonial system had been affected by the need of opposing the Colonial systems of rival Powers. Now she was free to take her own line, and to build up a great empire on a policy of her own.

Since that victory was won there has been an extraordinary expansion of British rule in America, in the Indies, in South Africa and in Australasia alike. It has been accompanied by the vigorous development of internal communications and natural resources; and still more by careful training in the art of self-government. It would be possible to quote figures which would serve to exhibit the rapidity of the expansion of area and of political and economical development; but surely on this centenary we should do well not to fix our attention on the extent of the growth, but to consider how far it has been sound, and therefore how far we may hope that it will continue to flourish. There are many aspects in which a great civilisation may be viewed, and many tests by which its stability may be gauged, but I shall only lay stress on one. Nothing seems to me so important as the religious factor in political life— the conscious recognition of the truth that except the Lord build the house their labour is but lost that build it, the habitual effort in public affairs to co-operate with Him.

Many influences have been at work during the last century, which have tended to the disparagement of this element in politics. The change cannot be entirely ascribed to increasing indifference, for it is partly the outcome of modern forms of religious earnestness. For one thing, the great evangelical movement has diffused an appreciation of the importance of religion as a personal thing in the heart, and (as some would say) as merely personal: religious opinions, religious practice, except as inspired by deep conviction, seem to be empty and worthless. On the other hand, the Indian administrator, in districts where there are many separate peoples, each with their own creed and each having a religion that seems to suit their needs, may find it hard to look on religion as a power that either invigorates or elevates political life. There may even be a temptation to resent the difficulties which religion sometimes causes, and to regard it almost as an evil in society. It may give rise to friction of many kinds, and it rarely seems in fact to re-enforce the doing of any political duty. Hence there is a widely current opinion, both in England and America, that a man may be an excellent citizen, whatever his opinions are, and even if he has no religion at all; that religion has nothing to do with the good government of the State, and that it is a matter about which the State may therefore be perfectly indifferent. Without pausing to discuss how far and under what limitations these opinions are true, or whether they are merely plausible, I think they may be cited as forms of the tendency to disparage religion as an element in the life of the Modern State. Against this tendency I desire to protest, since there are elements in the welfare of the State which are supplied by religion, and which cannot, so far as I see, be supplied in any other way. There are, at any rate, flaws and defects in political life which would be likely to show themselves more glaringly, if this influence, which can ennoble and invigorate the life of the State, were wholly withdrawn.

I. The recognition of Justice, as paramount, lies at the very foundation of all good government, and yet it is not easy to hold firmly to this conception of right in political affairs as above all considerations of expediency. Men are always apt to idolise any cause which they rate so highly that they are glad to make great personal sacrifices on its behalf. Some may be inclined to think of their order as a supreme aim in life, while others cleave to their country with the same unquestioning devotion. Those who thus overvalue any mundane institution are satisfied to note the conduct which is subservient to the aim they cherish, and are disinclined to inquire too curiously about right and wrong. Considerations of expediency

seem to be enough for practical guidance, while right
and justice can be dismissed as impracticable ideals,
they seem so shadowy. In the success of their
country such men seem to see the best they can aim
at, set before them in concrete form. But it is a
serious thing, under any pretence, however plausible,
to abandon ideals, and thus to give up the effort to
rise to a nobler level of practice than that on which
we happen to stand. So long as we retain high ideals
of Justice and Right, we can at least aim at them,
and we may possibly make some progress in the
effort to live up to them.

The nation of antiquity, who were most deeply
penetrated with this conception of an absolute righteousness as supreme, had received it and held to it
under a religious form. The history of Israel is
parallel to the history of other peoples in many ways :
their earlier story tells of the patriarch from whom
they were descended, and to whom they looked back
with reverence. But Abraham was not worshipped
by them as a tribal god who could be expected to
stand by his descendants and succour them when
they appealed to him ; he was the father of the
faithful. He had been called by a God, whose
promise was sure, on whom he could rely absolutely,
and the seed which sprang from him continued to
reverence this perfect Righteousness as directing their
destinies. This thought comes out at the beginning,
and it is even more marked at the close of the Old
Testament history. The conception of an absolute
right, as distinguished from the prosperity of the

realm, is insisted upon in the strongest fashion. The
prophets deplored, again and again, the departure of
the people from the law of God; they insisted that
He could not be expected to deliver His people,
merely because they were His people; but that the
men of Jerusalem, who sinned, should be punished for
their failure to live by God's law. The prophets re-
pudiated the maxims of struggling for one's country
—right or wrong,—and insisted that it was only as
the nation endeavoured to obey the absolute rule of
Divine Righteousness that they could look for Divine
countenance in their undertakings.

In modern times there is a tendency to abandon
this view, and to make it a test of patriotism that
men should follow what is expedient for their country,
without any attempt to consider what is right in
itself, or even what is fair to their neighbours. A
prominent American citizen has given terse expression
to this opinion. "Every decent Englishman," he
writes, "is devoted to his country, first, last and all
the time. An Englishman may or may not dislike
America, but he is invariably for England and against
America when any question arises between them;
and I heartily respect him for so being[1]." But
Englishmen would be the last to take credit to themselves for being mere partisans of their own country,
through thick and thin. It has been their pride that
they do endeavour to understand what is right, and
to give effect to it even at a great cost, in public
affairs of every kind. When there is no attempt to

[1] T. Roosevelt, *Administration—Civil Service*, p. 136.

maintain an ideal of right, as between nation and nation, there can be no meaning in such a phrase as a just war. If arbitration is to be a mere attempt to get the better of an opponent in a game of bluff, if it is conducted on either side by men who have failed to cultivate the sense of international fair play, there need be little surprise that it should be discredited as a sorry farce.

It is not only in international relations that there is need to hold fast to the idea of right, as absolute, but in the internal administration of public affairs as well. There is a tendency in all communities for some citizens to claim exceptional treatment, either as regards their obligations to the State, or in the manner in which government deals with them. The France of the *ancien régime* offers a stock example of a privileged class, who had immunity from taxation, and from whom it was difficult to obtain redress by process of law; but there are other communities in which plausible grounds can be alleged for granting special boons to particular persons, or classes or interests. Equality before the law is the basis of even-handed justice within the realm—the making of laws and the enforcing of laws without fear or favour. The tradition, established in this realm, of honest decisions by unbiassed tribunals is being diffused throughout the communities that come under English rule. Whatever blunders may have been committed in the great sub-continent which some of us recently visited with the British Association, it is at least a comfort to be assured that the people of all races have confidence in the administration of the law, and in the seriousness of the efforts made to do justly between man and man. When this is the case we may surely feel that the corner stone of a well-ordered society has been securely laid.

Both for good government within this realm, and for the maintenance of honourable relations with other communities, it is before all things necessary that there should be among Englishmen in the future, as there has been in the past, a recognition of right and justice as supreme over all particular aims and interests; and the simple theistic faith in which it seems to have originated, is surely the most potent instrument for maintaining this conviction effectively. The belief in one God, ruling over all the nations of the world, is common to all Christians—good, bad and indifferent—and to many non-Christians as well. The more firmly this ancient faith is held, the more ready may we be to lay all lesser aims aside, and to set ourselves to give effect to the perfectly Righteous Will in all the affairs of the Empire.

II. While it is well to maintain a high ideal, it is also essential in a well-ordered State that account should be taken of the particular conditions of the country and of the manner and extent to which right can be enforced. Government cannot be carried on unless there is such community of sentiment among the inhabitants that they respect the claims of the authority under which they live, and consent unto the law that it is good. Men of a similar stock, who have enjoyed similar political training through the influence of the same history, readily adopt an habitual attitude to government, as part of their national character. In the United States at present much pains is taken that, in spite of all the large accessions of aliens from outside, the national character shall not be tampered with, and that the national tradition shall be maintained. Not all of the would-be immigrants are capable of being assimilated into the community, and of being so moulded that they can live peaceably and contentedly in the American social system. The comparative ease, or difficulty, with which the men of different races can be assimilated to the habitual thought and sentiment of the typical American citizen, lies at the basis of the prohibition of Chinese immigration into the United States, and accounts for the doubtful welcome which is accorded to some of the Latin races.

The problem of maintaining a community of sentiment has to be faced in the old world as well as in the new; the great variety of racial and social types, which may be found among the citizens of the same country, greatly increases the difficulty of government, and especially of democratic government. In a country where each citizen has a voice in legislating for all the rest, there ought to be some similarity of habit and aspirations; if there are deeply-seated divergences of opinion as to the functions which the State should or should not undertake, there is danger on the one hand of the tyranny of a majority, and on the other of mere anarchy. Some of the tendencies at work among us seem to make for this last condition. We live in an age when individual self-assertion is tolerated as it has never been before ; the claims of the State upon the individual have been reduced to a minimum, while the opportunities for the individual to force his opinions on the State are unlimited. Those who cherish the ideal that every man should do "that which is right in his own eyes" cannot be good citizens, even if they do not develop a "genius for disobedience[1]." The jarring of separate interests and sentiments and opinions may disorganise society and leave it with no more cohesion than a rope of sand. When the people govern, some measure of agreement, and some willingness to subordinate particular aims to the commonweal are essential.

In the face of these difficulties, it is no light task to maintain a community of sentiment and a tradition of national character where it already exists ; to try and call it into being throughout large areas, peopled by men of different races, with mutually antagonistic sentiments, would seem to be hopeless altogether. But there is one force that can do it ; religion has a power of fundamentally changing personal sentiments and personal character ; of modifying them, so that they centre round another object than the individual personally. Religion can play a great part in the political sphere, by bringing about the assimilation of divers elements, and rendering life as one self-governing community, possible. Old Testament History affords vivid illustrations of success in attaining

[1] Bryce, *Impressions of South Africa*, p. 156.

to a united polity under the influence of common reverence for one God, and also of the disruptive forces which can be exercised by conflicting religious ordinances. Judaism had indeed comparatively little assimilative power in the time of the monarchy ; but it is the special claim of Christianity, apart from all the other religions of the world, that it sets itself to mould personal character. We are, as Christians, not encouraged to be self-assertive of our own opinions ; we are to bring every thought into captivity to the obedience of Christ. We are not to think too much of our own interests, since we must look not only on our own things but also on the things of others. The very purpose of Christ's gospel is to regenerate the individual and take him out of himself that he may be transformed by the renewing of his mind. Christ has a gospel, not only for the world to come, but for this present life—a word that can call into being a new earth. His religion can diffuse the atmosphere in which vigorous political life can grow and flourish. We should not grasp at the best Christianity has to offer, and be content to forego its lesser gifts. The life that Christ has brought among men is spiritual and eternal, but earthly blessings are added thereto. It has afforded, and it can still afford the community of thoughts and aims, the willingness to subordinate personal judgment and feeling, which are requisite for the successful conduct of civil government.

Christianity has this constraining character in a high degree, and it differs from all other religions

—notably from Mohammadanism—in the type of character it inculcates on citizens, either in the Kingdom of Heaven, or in the kingdoms of this world. It sets before us the man Christ Jesus. He stands unique and alone, for there is no type of merely national character which can be regarded as a model for all men and all ages. However inspiring as an example any other type of citizenship may be, there is none to which it is worth while consciously to conform, since there is none that man does not outgrow and get beyond. To set ourselves to live in the range of ideas and sentiments of the Greek citizen would be the merest affectation; nor is it possible that the intellectual standard of the eighteenth century, with its dogmas as to the natural rights of man, is the last word of political wisdom. There are new problems to be faced, and new experiences to be won in the sphere of political activity; we must take as the type of manhood we would wish to have in a political community, a model that we can never outgrow or hope to discard.

Since the first settlement of English colonists in distant parts of the world, and more systematically for the last two hundred years, Englishmen have made earnest efforts to foster the Christian faith of those who go out from this land and of their descendants in the new nations beyond the seas. This is a duty which is distinct from, but not less important than, the work of trying to convert and elevate the native races; there are some who hold that the missionary work of dealing with the heathen is most

likely to prosper, when the duty of fostering religious
life among those who are professedly Christian is put
in the forefront. We who live in a land where the
opportunities of Christian teaching and worship
are frequent, have little idea how easy it is for
religion to perish, from inanition, where distance
cuts men off from participation in Christian teaching
and Christian fellowship and Christian rites. The
governor of one of the New England States has
officially expressed his sense of the danger to which
the American rural population is exposed, and the
risk that they incur of lapsing into practical heathen-
ism ; and the difficulty of providing for Christian
observance, among the still more scattered population
of our Empire is far greater. At least, it is something
that Englishmen have carried with them the sense of
an obligation to face these difficulties. Souls are
things to be cared for, not to be left to care for themselves or not as they please. And in the South
African part of the Empire nothing impressed me
more than the pains which were being taken to keep
the scattered population in touch with Christian
teaching and Christian ordinances ; nothing struck
me as more remarkable than the response which these
efforts seemed to evoke. One specific case may serve as
an illustration ; and I venture to read a few sentences
from a letter which reached me since my return, from
the Archbishop of Capetown, who was visiting the
parish of Malmesbury,—an ecclesiastical district about
as extensive as Lincolnshire : " I have had," he
writes, " a very interesting fortnight, though a very

tiring one of almost perpetual motion, but a wonderful amount of encouragement. In one place I dedicated a little stone church, built almost entirely by the manual labours and self-denying alms of the fishing families there, with a population in all of about 175. Towards this building they had given £83 in money and £150 in labour. At the dedication service they said they were determined to pay off the debt of £44; and the collection was £53, of which over £40 was contributed by themselves. Out of 175, men, women, and little ones, 94 communicated. I am told not one single case of drunkenness or immorality has taken place there for ten years, and there is a perfectly wonderful spirit of charity and kindliness among the people. It is like a little community of early Christians, though free from persecution." Thus it is that in spite of the difficulties, eager efforts are being made to give free course to those religious influences which, apart from their directly spiritual aspects, can so mould human character as to make possible the growth of a flourishing political organism.

As we look back from the centenary of Trafalgar we may surely thank God and take courage. Great self-governing nations have come into being in all the corners of the globe, since that victory was gained, and English influence was rendered paramount on the high seas. There are many who are ready to judge us, nor need we resent it, since we can always learn something from criticism, however unfriendly it may be. But after all, the political life of this Empire is not destitute of those redeeming elements which religion supplies. Most of us hold fast to the faith of the Old Testament—that in political life there is a standard of right which rises far above all dictates of expediency, and all mere partisanship. Many of us hold enthusiastically to the faith of the New Testament,—that human nature may be so moulded that each citizen shall be less eager to assert his rights, and each more ready to serve his fellow-men for Christ's sake. These convictions are the gift of God; so long as we consciously look to Him for an increase of His gifts, we may confidently hope that He will continue to use this English people as His instrument for introducing civilised life, for ennobling human nature, and for diffusing the love of God and His Righteousness throughout the world.

THE IMPERIALISM OF CROMWELL.

THE foundations of the English Empire were laid during the seventeenth century. When that era opened, there were no established trading connections between this country and the East, and some fishing rights in Newfoundland constituted our only territorial claims in the West. Before it closed, however, the East India Company had obtained a firm footing in Bombay, Madras, and Bengal, and had already entered on its career of conquest. We had some possessions on the Guinea coast, and held Jamaica, Barbados, and other West Indian Islands, while our colonies stretched in an unbroken line on the Atlantic seaboard from Florida to Canada. The rapid growth of these distant possessions is a demonstration of the extraordinary enterprise which Englishmen were showing both in commerce and colonisation. Mercantile activity has always served as a pioneer and has extended our political influence in all parts of the globe, even though naval or military expeditions have subsequently been necessary to hold and maintain the positions occupied by cultivators and traders. The bases of the British Empire were laid in the seventeenth century; this was its lasting achievement, and the work was accomplished by men who were strongly influenced by economic motives.

It is equally true that one figure stands out in the history of England during the seventeenth century as unique. There is something extraordinarily dramatic in the rise of Oliver Cromwell from a position of comparative obscurity to supreme authority not only in the Army, but in the State also. He has been described by Professor Gardiner as a typical Englishman; and some who doubt whether the traits which mark his character are widely diffused in the present day, would yet assert that his life was thoroughly typical of the dominant political and religious forces of the middle of the seventeenth century in England. It seems to follow, almost as a matter of course, that he should be expected to take a leading part in the work of colonisation and commercial expansion and empire building, which was the principal achievement of the age from which he drew his inspiration and on which he left so deep a mark. Recent writers have vied with one another in attributing to him a keen interest in economic progress and the consequent expansion of England. Dr Beer, of Columbia College, who has studied the later policy of England towards the American colonies most carefully, lays stress on this element in connection with Cromwell's expedition to the West Indies: "Economic motives were the cause, religious motives the justification of the West Indian project. . . . In fighting Spain, Cromwell believed that he was fighting the Lord's battles. But there can be no doubt that these battles would never have been fought, if victory in them would not have added to England power and greatness[1]." Seeley's judgment, "That notions of trade seem at most but secondary in his mind" is dismissed with scorn as based "on a lack of knowledge of the facts," since, according to Dr Beer, the fundamental motives for the expedition were "economic." Mr Wolf, in his interesting monograph on the re-admission of the Jews, is even more decided in his statement.

The Re-admission of the Jews to England was one of Cromwell's own schemes,—part and parcel of that dream of Imperial expansion which filled his later days with its stupendous administration and vanished so tragically with his early death—it is impossible to doubt....Cromwell's statecraft was, as I have said, not entirely or even essentially governed by religious policy. He desired to make England great and prosperous as well as pious and free.... The Jews could not but appeal to him as very desirable instruments for his colonial and commercial policy[2].

Sir William Hunter expresses the same view in a forcible fashion : "As he set himself, while still a cavalry colonel, to form an army of victory at home, so he resolved, as head of the Commonwealth, to create a marine which should give England predominance abroad. The Navigation Act of 1651 served as his new model for winning the supremacy of the seas[3]."

In the face of these confident assertions I venture

---

[1] *Quarterly Review of Political Science* (New York), xvi. 608–11.

[2] *Manasseh Ben Israel's Mission to Oliver Cromwell*, Introduction, p. xxix.

[3] *History of British India*, ii. 107.

to put forward a few reasons for thinking that Seeley's insight did not play him false in this matter, and that Cromwell was but little concerned with the progress in commerce and colonisation which brought about the expansion of England.

In the first place it is worth while to point out that there was during this period no marked development of trade policy. Various steps were taken under the Council of State and the Protectorate for the benefit of English commerce, and we may, if we like, ascribe them to the personal influence of Cromwell, though there does not seem to be much ground for doing so. There is, for example, no evidence that Cromwell had anything to do with the passing of the Navigation Act. On the day when he was writing his well-known despatch about the "crowning mercy" at Worcester, the House was sitting in Committee on the Bill which had already passed its second reading; he did not join the Committee on Trade till some weeks later. A contemporary writer regarded him as out of sympathy with the policy of the measure. Roger Coke held that the Navigation Act was merely mischievous in its effects on English trade; but, much as he disliked Cromwell, he makes the grudging admission that "Old Oliver looked coldly" upon it and constantly set it aside by granting licences[1]. But whether Cromwell directed the trade policy of the Commonwealth or not, it is worth while to point out that no evidence has been brought forward which shows

[1] *Discourse of Trade* (1670), p. 22.

that the authorities during the Interregnum entertained new ideas as to the line that ought to be pursued. The Civil War in England had led to a considerable disturbance of trade, and the execution of the King had raised a scandal which rendered the position of English merchants in France, Spain, Portugal, and other countries exceedingly difficult; while royalist privateers, and the ships of other nations preyed upon English commerce. The resentment in Russia was so keen that trading relations were broken off by the Czar, and the hostility of the Spaniards was very injurious. The footing which English merchants had purchased for themselves in Andalusia in 1645 was lost, and it was not till after the Restoration in (1667) that their privileges were so enlarged and extended that they had any chance of competing there with the Dutch. To this extent at all events the Protector failed to recover the ground which had been lost during the troubles at home.

It is of course true that Cromwell had control of a much finer navy than was possessed by Charles the First, but it would be a mistake to suppose that that monarch was either indifferent to the maintenance of maritime power or careless about the protection of merchant-shipping. The necessity of repelling the attacks of Algerian pirates had been the reason put forward for levying Ship-money, and there are constant references in the State Papers to the employment of royal ships on convoy service. The troubles connected with the Civil War greatly increased the risk to traders, but it does not seem that the Council of State, though they gave some attention to the subject in 1650, were successful in supplying adequate protection even to vessels engaged in the coasting trade. The attempt to provide convoys for the Levant trade was costly, while an occasional raid, like Blake's attack on the nest of pirates at Tunis, only seems to have increased the ordinary risks of English trade in these parts. Many dismal complaints of loss were made during the last years of the Protectorate; and it was only after the Restoration that an effective convoy system at moderate rates was organised, so as to enable the English merchant to compete with the Dutch.

Cromwell was more fortunate in his dealings with Portugal, and he negotiated a treaty which was of importance to English merchants. With the restoration of the House of Braganza in 1640, the Portuguese territories in Brazil and settlements in India were cut off from Spanish influence; it was important that English merchants should have a favourable reception at Lisbon, and be free to engage in the distant trades for which Portuguese shipping did not suffice, as well as in the carrying trade in European waters. There was an ancient amity between the Crowns of England and of Portugal, and in 1642 Charles the First had completed a treaty which renewed the old relations and gave English merchants a satisfactory footing. Not unnaturally the King of Portugal favoured the royalist cause, and gave shelter and assistance to Prince Rupert in the time of the Commonwealth. It was a triumph for the diplomacy of the Protector that he was able to heal the breach that had arisen and to obtain the restoration of the English merchants to a position similar to, though not so favourable as, that which Charles had secured for them; but in this there was nothing new.

From the time of Queen Elizabeth, to go no farther back, English rulers had endeavoured to obtain access to the Baltic trade on favourable terms, —especially as regards the tolls exacted at the Sound. Cromwell was successful in negotiating with Denmark to obtain the concession that the English should pay no higher tolls than those demanded of the most favoured nation. It does not appear, however, that the English were able to take much advantage of this turn of affairs; there was a lack of shipping suitable for the Baltic trade, and the Navigation Act of 1651 had made it impossible to import timber and naval stores in Dutch bottoms. So great was the mischief accruing to the maritime interest of the realm from the deficiency of these commodities that it was necessary to relax the provisions of the Navigation Act over and over again; but the Muscovy trade, the Eastland trade, and the Northern trades do not seem to have developed to any extent under the Protectorate, or even to have recovered the measure of prosperity they had enjoyed under Charles.

Those, however, who insist on Cromwell's eagerness to promote maritime and Imperial interests do not profess to rest their case so much on what he actually accomplished as on the policy which was adopted while he had a prominent place in public affairs. The Navigation Act of 1651 has often been said to mark a turning-point in the relative position of England and Holland on the seas. It was passed with the definite intention of attacking the Dutch supremacy in the commerce of the world, and under its ægis English shipping did certainly increase until, in the course of the eighteenth century, it outstripped that of Holland altogether. How far the Act in question contributed to this result it is difficult to say; partly because it is clear that for considerable periods it was not enforced, and that its operation was occasionally suspended. Constant complaints have come down to us as to its mischievous effects on English trade, and all that we are able to say is that the experts who persisted in maintaining its principles, and who tried to put them in practice, were probably better informed as to its working than anyone can be in the present day. We may come, with some hesitation, to the conclusion that it benefited English shipping, and to that extent did some negative injury to Holland; the Dutch did not in all probability increase as much as they would have done. But there is no evidence that it inflicted more than a temporary inconvenience or that it caused positive injury to the United Provinces. The commerce and industry of the country continued to advance till the middle of the eighteenth century; the energy of the Dutch may have been deflected from ocean voyages to those nearer trades which

Adam Smith deemed to be more profitable. But apart altogether from the difficult question as to how far this measure served its purpose and injured the Dutch, there is little reason to suppose that the policy was a new departure. Navigation Acts of one sort or another had been in operation at various dates from the time of Richard the Second; in the time of Elizabeth the expedient of limiting commerce to English ships had been somewhat discredited, as it was found that it provoked counter-restrictions in other lands and might reduce commercial intercourse to a deadlock. James the First had remitted the consideration of the subject to his Council of Trade in 1622, and it certainly assumed a new importance with the growth of the tobacco and sugar colonies in Virginia and the West Indies. These plantations, which were not utilised for subsistence farming but for the growth of valuable commodities for export, had been founded and were maintained with the help of the capital of English merchants, and it seemed fair that they should have a first claim to the profits that might accrue from the commerce. During the war with France, Charles the First had been in favour of allowing other ships to be employed[1]; but the intrusion of Dutch merchants became so general that in 1637 he adopted another policy and endeavoured to drive the Hollanders out of the trade altogether. He enjoined the Governor of Virginia to "strictly and resolutely to forbid all trade or trading with any Dutch ship that shall either purposely or casually

[1] Sept. 5, 1627: Hist. MSS. Com., iii. 69.

come to any of your plantations." If, however, in extremity they made an exception he insisted that "good caution and bond be taken both by the Dutch master as also of the owners of the said tobacco and other commodities so laden that they shall without fraud be brought to our port of London." Here we have the principle of the Navigation Act as regards both ships and commodities; and a proclamation of 1629 also anticipates that measure in applying similar restrictions to the Eastland trade.

Under these circumstances it is difficult to admit the claim made on behalf of Cromwell, or to recognise that he exercised any very great influence on the economic development and expansion of England. Commercial affairs do not seem to have prospered greatly under his rule, and the measures which he took in regard to them were for the most part directly borrowed from the system of Charles. We are able to press the argument a little further, however, and to show that he was half-hearted or careless about matters that were essential to the growth of English maritime power, and that his ideas, so far from being in advance of those of his contemporaries, were actually retrograde.

The Tudors and the Stuarts had endeavoured to direct commercial intercourse into channels which might promote the maritime strength of England as a fighting Power. The gravest defect in the Navigation Act was its application to the Baltic trade, since it seems to have caused an interruption of the ordinary means of communication and increased the difficulty of procuring naval stores; and Cromwell showed a curious disregard of another element of national strength. The best hope of obtaining a supply of saltpetre and having the means of making gunpowder lay in the development of the East India trade. James and Charles had both been eagerly interested in the supply of saltpetre; they did not indeed show any great enthusiasm for strengthening the monopoly of the East India Company, and they frequently exercised their power of authorising particular voyages on the part of independent traders. Cromwell's position was very different; he aspired to ape the pretensions of Alexander the Third, and proposed to divide the world between the two maritime Protestant Powers. His suggestion was that the Dutch should withdraw from America, and that Englishmen should abandon their position in the East. So far was he from promoting the expansion of commercial enterprise that he was prepared to limit English shippers to one hemisphere, and to let the country become dependent on our chief antagonist for its main supply of powder. Such a scheme would hardly have been put forward by a man who was either alive to the advantage of commercial progress, or sensitive as to the economic conditions of national power; when the plan for withdrawing from the Indies altogether fell to the ground, his Council of Trade recommended strengthening the status of the Company so that it might fight its own battles in the East.

His ideas on colonisation are still more curious.

Under James and Charles the planting of the American coast had gone steadily forward; the Governments were strongly in favour of the project in both reigns, as they recognised that a new England beyond the seas would be an effective check on the dominance of Spanish influence, and would in itself add to the credit and prestige of this country. The English emigrants were not content to establish factories for trade, as the Dutch did at New Amsterdam and the French at Montreal; still less were they content merely to mine. The constant object in view was the reproduction of a new rural England, with some large estates and many yeomen farmers. The policy of the Government was clear; they wished to avoid the mistake the Spaniards had made in establishing settlements which could only procure the necessaries of life by trade. The English colonies were planted in the expectation that after the first year or two they would be able to grow the means of their own subsistence, and not be dependent on the advent of an occasional ship for sufficient food. The Northern colonies, round Massachusetts Bay, were devoted to subsistence farming, and caused no trouble in this respect; but Virginia, the capitalist colony in the South, was in a different case. The London merchants who financed it, and the planters themselves, found it easier to devote all their energies to growing tobacco for export, and the Governments of James and Charles had to put repeated pressure on them to develope the production of cereals so that their economic existence might be secure even in the event of a war with

Spain. But Cromwell was entirely careless in this matter ; after the conquest of Jamaica he tried to induce the New Englanders to migrate from their plantations in the North to his new acquisition, and others were urged to return to Ireland. He would have sacrificed the hold which England had on the Northern seaboard, and the well-established subsistence farming there, for the development of an island in which commodities could be produced for export. He deliberately abandoned the sound lines on which English colonisation was proceeding, and proposed to imitate the Spanish system, the weakness of which had been patent for fifty years. It is surely unreasonable to ascribe to Cromwell a large share in fostering colonial expansion, when his views on the subject were so retrograde.

It does not seem to me that any of the rulers of England in the seventeenth century played a conspicuous part in the commercial and colonial development which was the only striking feature of the times. "It had its spring," Mr Morley says truly, "in the abiding demands of national circumstance, in the continuous activity of economic necessities upon a national character of incomparable energy and adventure. Such a policy was not and could not be the idea of one man, or the mark of a single generation[1]." Its success was almost entirely due to the enterprise of private citizens either acting personally, or when associated in companies. But after all, the sanction of Government was needed for

[1] *Oliver Cromwell*, by John Morley, p. 448.

the initiation of new schemes, and it may be said of the Stuarts, both before and after the Interregnum, that their attitude was both intelligent and sympathetic. They were entirely free from that jealousy of colonial development which came out so markedly in the Parliaments of the later seventeenth and the eighteenth centuries. They approved of colonisation as raising English prestige, and while they were concerned to strengthen the political connection with the mother country they did not take pains to hamper, though they might direct, economic development. They were besides careful to take the advice of experts, and in colonial matters they appear to have followed the views of Captain John Smith, whose *Advice to Young Planters* seems thoroughly sensible when read in the light of the subsequent history of colonisation. He possibly was not strictly veracious when recounting his own dealings with the Indians, and he had his prejudices; he did not think much of the gentlemen in London who directed the affairs of Virginia from their board-room in the City; but James and Charles, possibly under his influence, played an exceedingly sensible and cordial part in these matters, in so far as they interfered. Of Cromwell it may be enough to say that when once liberty of conscience was sufficiently established in England itself, he seems to have felt that the main reason for migrating to new shores was gone, and that the action he took towards the colonists in suggesting another removal was neither sympathetic nor intelligent.

On these various grounds I venture to reiterate
Seeley's view that notions of trade did not play a
large part in Cromwell's policy.   Seeley undoubtedly
wrote, as we all must, without full knowledge of the
facts; but it seems to me that the more the facts
are studied, the more fully is Seeley's opinion justified,
and it is supported by the judgment of Mr Morley.
I will only indicate two confirmatory lines of argument, on which I do not enter.   The commercial and
colonising interests in London were so strong that,
if Cromwell's policy had been really favourable to
them, it is inconceivable that the City men should
have thwarted him so much, and been so ready to
welcome back the Stuarts;   the movement which
culminated in the Restoration is utterly incompre-
hensible if it was rolling on and accumulating force
in the teeth of the economic interests of the nation.
Once more, the extraordinary development which
occurred in the last half of the seventeenth century
has no direct connection with the lines of policy laid
down by Cromwell.   He was eager to oppose Spain;
the course of progress which ultimately triumphed
was inspired by jealousy of that trade with France
which he had done so much to encourage.

So little evidence can be adduced in behalf of the
view that Cromwell was keenly interested in colonial
and commercial expansion, that it is worth while
to enquire how the opinion should have arisen and
obtained such general popularity in recent years.
There is, of course, the antecedent probability that
the typical strong man of the seventeenth century

would have a part in the special development which
characterised the England of that period. But there
are other reasons; there can, I think, be no doubt
that Cromwell was extraordinarily eager to obtain
such conditions for the Jews that they might be
attracted to settle in England, and his leanings to
a commercial race have been interpreted as proving
that he cherished commercial ambitions for his
country. But his pro-Semitic bias is susceptible
of a much simpler explanation; the chosen people
appealed alike to his deepest sentiments and to his
personal interests as Protector. The Jews were the
victims of Spanish tyranny, and that would of itself
constitute a claim to Cromwell's support. But besides
this, the Government was in great want of money,
and the wealthy Dutch Jews had plenty of money
to lend. It had become a usual practice for Government to borrow in the ordinary course of affairs, but
the system was not yet organised. There was no
State Bank like that of Genoa, and the City magnates
were in no hurry to come forward and aid the head
of the Army by establishing one. There was an
increasing difficulty in collecting taxes or obtaining
supplies, and Cromwell was not unnaturally ready to
curry favour with the Jews of Holland, and at least
to divert them from lending assistance to the Royalist
cause. Spanish Crypto-Jews resident in London had
already conferred a similar service on the Parlia-
mentary party, and Cromwell's best chance of tiding
over his pressing pecuniary difficulties lay in granting
political status to and receiving help from the Jews.

For his patronage of their forefathers succeeding
generations of Jews have always been grateful, and
their historians in the present day are ready to
attribute to him the virtues they most admire, and
to paint him as a keen and far-seeing business man.
He had so many activities that no two biographers
are likely to lay stress on the same quality. Carlyle
admired him as a great general, an autocrat with
many statesmanlike powers, and a deeply religious
man. It may be worth while to add that he showed
business shrewdness in the practical matters, such as
the draining of the fens, which fell within his own
personal knowledge. It is, however, quite consistent
with this view of his character to hold that when
in power he seized the chance to make an attack on
the political and religious system of Spain, without
much regard to the injury thereby inflicted on the
industrial and commercial classes. But to treat him
as an ardent expansionist and to explain his action
as due to economic aspirations, is to injure his reputation by injudicious praise, since this view of
his conduct is likely to raise doubts both as to his
common-sense and his sincerity. One panegyrist has
written :

The statesmen of the Commonwealth, who knew so well
how to conjure with human enthusiasm, were essentially
practical men. To imagine that they were the slaves of
the great religious revival which had enabled them to
overcome the loyalist inspiration of the cavaliers is entirely to misconceive their character and aims. The logical
outcome of that revival, and of the triumph of the Puritan
arms, would have been the Kingdom of Saints, but Crom-

well's ambition aimed at something much more conventional. Imperial expansion and trade ascendency filled a larger place in his mind than the Other-worldly inspirations which had carried him to power [1].

I almost think that Oliver would have regarded the scurrility of Royalist pamphleteers, who commented on his improved fortunes, as less offensive than the lavish praise of the enthusiasts of the twentieth century.

There are, moreover, political reasons which have rendered this strained interpretation of Cromwell's aims and character particularly attractive in the present day. The Anglo-Saxon race has entered, in both its leading branches, on a great era of expansion. Roosevelt in America and Rosebery in England are names that stand out in connection with the New Imperialism ; but there has been a difficulty in the matter. The Anglo-Saxon mind loves a precedent, and the political records on either side of the Atlantic yielded little that could be used by democrats in support of the new departure. Royalists and courtiers had been more commonly concerned in promoting expansion. Washington's charge to his nation seemed to exclude it altogether from American statesmanship; the British Liberal tradition told of much indifference to the colonies in the nineteenth century and no little jealousy of them in the eighteenth, but it scarcely yielded a name that could be quoted as that of an enthusiast for expansion, till it was discovered that Cromwell could be used to fill the vacant niche

[1] Wolf, *op. cit.* p. xxviii.

and pose as the patron saint of Liberal Imperialism. He has served the purpose admirably; Lord Rosebery has unveiled his statue for the nation, and President Roosevelt has written his life. Such appreciation is instructive, since it throws an interesting light on the views of the politicians who point to their hero as a model. Liberal Imperialism has been somewhat vague and ill-defined, and there is a satisfaction in getting a concrete presentment of the ideals of its leaders. Cromwell was before all else efficient; efficient in his organisation of the Army, efficient in his treatment of the Navy, and particularly efficient in his dealings with the native Irish. He had no patience with the inefficiency of his predecessors; they had attempted, in the plantation of Ireland, to introduce such an admixture of English inhabitants that civil order might be established and economic progress might become possible, without unnecessarily interfering with the old inhabitant. The Cromwellian method of settlement was much simpler; the greater part of the native population was deported to the bleak area between the Shannon and the Galway coast, while large numbers were carried off to be employed in miserable servitude in Jamaica and the sugar plantations. It is easy enough to be efficient in such circumstances, but only if you are prepared to be utterly ruthless. At all events Cromwell had the courage of his opinions and was not satisfied to saunter along a primrose path; but the failure of his *régime* may give us pause. The problem of governing two races on the same soil is most likely to be solved

by men who do not rely on heroic measures; they
must be ready to learn by experience, and be on the
alert to use such opportunities for improvement as
occur.   This was the course pursued by the Stuart
kings, and the results of their rule contrast not un-
favourably with the heritage of race-hatred which has
associated itself with the name of Cromwell.

Printed in the United States
By Bookmasters